P.O. BOX 223

NEWTOWN SQUARE, P.A. 19073

The Political Theory of Anarchism

The Political Theory of Anarchism

April Carter

A TORCHBOOK LIBRARY EDITION
Harper & Row, Publishers
New York, Evanston, San Francisco, London

This book was first published in 1971 by Routledge and Kegan Paul Ltd., London and is here reprinted by arrangement.

THE POLITICAL THEORY OF ANARCHISM.

First TORCHBOOK LIBRARY EDITION published 1971.

STANDARD BOOK NUMBER (cloth): 06-136050-3

LIBRARY OF CONGRESS CATALOG CARD NUMBER: 73-162289

Contents

4 Anarchism and the Individual   89

The Egoist
The Artist
The Moralist
The Hero
The Coward
The Political Realm
The Citizen

Acknowledgments

I am very grateful to Geoffrey Ostergaard, Nigel Young, Margaret Leslie and to my sister Fay for encouragement, criticism and advice on this manuscript at various stages. Their comments have saved me from many errors; those remaining are my own responsibility.

Introduction

The cluster of ideas, attitudes and beliefs which can be defined by the term 'anarchism' have not received much attention from political theorists. There are a number of reasons for this neglect. One is that anarchist political theory sounds like a contradiction in terms—a denial of the value and necessity of government both sweeps aside many of the traditional concerns of political theorists, and suggests an essentially apolitical doctrine. Another is the lack of any outstanding theoretical exponent of anarchism. There are important, interesting and attractive anarchist writers, but none comparable as social theorists with, for example, Marx. Within the corpus of 'great political thinkers' only Rousseau comes close occasionally to being an anarchist. A third reason for the comparative neglect of anarchism is probably the fact that anarchists have never yet won permanent victory, and there are no anarchist societies in being; so their opponents have never felt under pressure to examine anarchist ideas very seriously. However, their political failure is also the anarchists' strength, as spokesmen for values which the politically established and victorious have too often forgotten or suppressed.

Anarchism like most other contemporary political ideals and doctrines began to emerge as a relatively coherent theory at about the time of the French Revolution. William Godwin's *Political Justice*, which is usually treated as the first theoretical exposition of anarchism, was popularly regarded as a reply to Burke's denunciation of the Revolution. Godwin was writing within the theoretical framework of individualism and rationalism associated with the eighteenth century Enlightenment. The diversity of anarchist thought is illustrated by the fact that the next major anarchist theorist, Max Stirner, belonged to the generation of young intellectuals in Germany of the 1840s who were strongly influenced by Hegel's Idealist philosophy, and who developed their own theories through a systematic critique of the more conservative implications of Hegel's philosophy in relation to the State and to religion. Another member of that circle of Young Hegelians, Karl Marx, later attacked the ideas of the other Young Hegelians, including those of 'Saint Max', in *The German Ideology*. Stirner argued in *The Ego and His Own* that the individual should be totally free from all socially imposed ties and from the conventions of morality. Godwin and Stirner had in common only their atheism and their willingness to take to logical extremes the belief that the individual—not the State or Society—is sovereign. In their stress on the complete autonomy of the individual both differed from most later anarchist thinkers. By the second half of the nine-teenth century anarchism had become a political movement closely associated with the international socialist movement, and sharing to some extent the socialist commitment to fraternity as a social ideal, and working class solidarity as a necessary weapon in the political struggle.

The development of anarchism as a political movement revealed that it was a doctrine which had its strongest appeal in areas where the process of industrialization had not yet changed the social land-scape: among craftsmen like the Swiss watchmakers in the Jura mountains; among skilled workers in small factories, as in France in the 1860s; and among poverty-stricken peasants, for example in Andalusia in Spain. The type of anarchism developed by Pierre-Joseph Proudhon, who first adopted the title 'anarchist', idealized the sturdy independence of the small peasant proprietor or skilled craftsman, and proposed a type of co-operative organization appropriate to the economic needs of this kind of community and to a society of in-dependent equals. Proudhon had spent part of his childhood on a farm in the Franche-Comté, was apprenticed as a printer (a trade which has produced many anarchists), and gained some of his ideas—in-cluding the name of his 'Mutualist' social and economic theory—from the militant textile workers of Lyons in the 1840s. His thought always tended to reflect these models of society, though he extended his theory to include workers' co-operative ownership of large scale industry. For a time the Proudhonists were a significant force in the French socialist movement, and in the First Socialist International, which was founded in 1864, the year before Proudhon's death.

But the dominant anarchist figure of the First International was the Russian Michael Bakunin, a genuinely internationalist revolution-ary who saw the inside of a great many European jails. Bakunin's influence was greatest in Switzerland, where for a short time the headquarters of his separate anarchist international was located; and in particular among the Jura watchmakers, whom he had encouraged in their initiative in opposing Marx's leadership of the First Inter-national. The Jura watchmakers epitomized the virtues of the Proud-honian ideal. Bakunin's compatriot, Prince Peter Kropotkin, said in his *Memoirs* that the Jura watchmakers had finally converted him to anarchism.

The very organization of the watch trade, which permits men to know one another thoroughly and to work in their own houses,

where they are free to talk, explains why the level of intellectual
development in this population is higher than that of workers
who spend all their life from early childhood in the factories.
There is more independence and more originality among petty
trades ... The clearness of insight, the soundness of judgment, the
capacity for disentangling complex social questions, which I
noticed amongst these workers ... deeply impressed me; ... But
the equalitarian relations which I found ... appealed even more
strongly to my feelings (266-7).

Bakunin, however, saw himself rather as the spokesman for the
very poor: the 'proletariat of the countryside, this last outcast of
history', and 'that great mass, those millions of non-civilized, dis-
inherited, wretched and illiterates' who are 'very nearly unpolluted
by all bourgeois civilization' (*Marxism, Freedom and the State*, 47-8).
Bakunin tried to win support in Italy, but had more success among
workers in the towns of the northern-central provinces than among
the very poor peasants of the South. In Spain, however, Bakunin's
Italian emissary, Fanelli, was successful in spreading anarchism not
only among the workers but among the rural proletariat. Bakunin's
concern for the poorest peasants, and for the 'riff raff', was not intended to exclude other potentially revolutionary groups. Bakunin
often seems to share Marx's belief that the factory workers will be in
the vanguard of revolutionary activity—at least in the West; and
he saw the potentialities of the strike as a revolutionary tactic. What
Bakunin objected to was Marx's exclusive emphasis on the organized
working class, because this approach ignored the possibility of revolt
by other groups, and because it seemed to imply a new 'class domination' over the masses, the peasantry and 'lumpenproletariat'.

Bakunin's thought had affinities with Proudhon, whom he had
read and admired; though Bakunin, consistent with his appeal to the
propertyless and illiterate, opposed personal ownership of property
in land or of small workshops, and what he regarded as the bourgeois
ideology of individualism. Instead he urged a form of 'collectivism':

I think that liberty must establish itself in the world by the
spontaneous organisation of labour and of collective ownership by
productive associations freely organised and federalised in
districts ... (*Marxism, Freedom and the State*, 18).

Kropotkin, before he encountered the Jura watchmakers, had
already been inclined towards anarchism by his experience on the
one hand of the brutality, corruption and incompetence of the Tsarist
régime; and on the other by his perception of the natural good sense,
initiative, and ability for spontaneous co-operation among the 'un-

civilized' tribes in Siberia, or among the Russian peasantry. His perceptions and his conclusions were similar to those formed by the other eminent Russian anarchist theorist, Count Leo Tolstoy. Kropotkin observed in his *Memoirs*:

> The years that I spent in Siberia taught me many lessons which I could hardly have learned elsewhere. I soon realised the absolute impossibility of doing anything really useful for the masses of the people by the means of the administrative machinery . . . To witness for instance, the ways in which the communities of the Dukhobortsy . . . migrated to the Amur region; to see the immense advantages which they got from their semi-communistic brotherly organization; and to realise what a success their colonization was, amidst all the failures of State colonization, was learning something which cannot be learned from books . . . The part which the unknown masses play in the accomplishment of all important historical events, and even in war, became evident to me from direct observation, and I came to hold ideas similar to those which Tolstoy expresses concerning the leaders and the masses in his monumental work, *War and Peace* (201–2).

Intellectuals in Russia were particularly attracted to anarchist ideas, both because existing social and economic conditions seemed favourable to the transition to an anarchist society—the Russian peasant commune as a basis for a regenerated society appealed to many radicals—and because throughout most of the nineteenth century and early twentieth century the existing government barred the way to moderate liberal reforms. However Russian anarchists had surprisingly little mass revolutionary support. George Woodcock comments in his study of *Anarchism* that only 'between 1918 and 1921, did Russian anarchists gain a brief and sudden glory when the peasants of the southern Ukraine flocked in their tens of thousands to the black banners of the anarchist guerilla leader Nestor Makhno', whose army was crushed by Trotsky in 1921 (376).

Bakunin in his polemic with Marx about the organization and policy of the First International, and about the role of the State after a socialist revolution, contrasted the anarchist tendencies of the Latin and Slav nations with German authoritarianism. Although such generalizations should, as Bakunin was aware, be treated with caution, his predictions were not inaccurate. Germany had become by 1900 the home of the best organized and best drilled Marxist Party in Europe. The German anarchist Gustav Landauer complained in 1896 in a report to the London International Congress that : 'in no other country has a single party, an isolated sect, managed to such a degree to pass for the unique and only legitimate representative of the proletariat . . .' (*Social Democracy in Germany*, 1). But anarchist ideas retained popularity in France, Italy, Russia and Spain well into this century, even after the progress of industrialization, and the organization of significant Marxist movements in these countries. In France, the most industrially advanced, Proudhonian Mutualism was adapted to the realities of large scale industry in the form of anarcho-syndicalism, which looked to a federal trade union organization as the basis for revolutionary action, and for administration in a future socialist society. This conception had been foreshadowed in Proudhon's own views on the need for workers' productive co-operatives to run factories, and in his insistence that the workers should avoid the snares of parliamentary politics and concentrate on building up their economic strength. Syndicalism was also influenced by Bakunin's more militant and collectivist anarchism. But syndicalism as it developed was not always linked to anarchist theory, and many anarchists had reservations about the syndicalist emphasis on working exclusively through trade union organizations.

Anarchists who did not espouse syndicalism tended by the end of the nineteenth century to embrace the doctrine of anarchist communism. Kropotkin was the best known exponent of anarchist communism, which differed from Bakuninist collectivism in seeking the abolition of the wage system and of all forms of private property. One of the most outstanding anarchists who advocated anarchist communism was the Italian Errico Malatesta, active between the 1870s and the 1920s. Malatesta combined Kropotkin's belief in complete communal ownership of property with a Marxist reliance on the organized political strength of the working class, and drew to some extent from both belief in a historically determined socialist future. He later came to believe that he had been both too Marxist and too Kropotkinian (see Vernon Richards, ed, *Errico Malatesta: His Life and Ideas*, 209–10). He sympathized with the Italian experiment in anarcho-syndicalism which, inspired by the French example, won support among railway, building and metal workers in northern cities just before the First World War; though he differed enough from the syndicalists to try to revive the anarchist movement between 1913–14. After the War the anarchists supported the 1919–20 movement towards workers' occupation and control of the factories, a movement inspired by the example of the Russian Soviets. The anarchists themselves initially hailed the Bolshevik régime, though by November 1921 they were formally denouncing Lenin's Bolshevik Government as the major enemy of the Revolution (see Daniel Guérin, *L'Anarchisme*, 131). After Mussolini's advent to power anarchist organizations in Italy were effectively crushed.

In the Soviet Union itself many anarchists initially supported the
October Revolution, but soon began to oppose aspects of the régime.
Anarchists split on the question of whether to support the Bolshevik
Government during the Civil War. Up to 1921 both anarcho-syndicalist and anarchist groups continued to be active, despite considerable police harassment—some anarchists had turned to armed
resistance and terrorist tactics, and though Lenin had distinguished
between these groups and ideological anarchists in general, the
political police, the Cheka, did not. By the end of 1922 anarchist
groups and propaganda had been eliminated much more successfully
than by the Tsarist régime. In 1921 and 1922 the Cheka shot many
anarchists, including the pacifist Tolstoyans. Kropotkin had hastened
back from exile after the February Revolution in 1917. He defended
the new Bolshevik régime against attacks from abroad, but protested
against the Government's suppression of all non-Communist publica-
tions, and its practice of taking hostages. Kropotkin's views on
developments in Russia are described briefly by another Russian born
anarchist who returned after the Revolution, Emma Goldman, in her
book *My Disillusionment with Russia*. Kropotkin died in February
1921. The mile-long procession through the streets of Moscow that
marked his funeral was the last public anarchist demonstration in
Russia.

Anarchism has persisted more tenaciously in Spain than in other
countries. In the nineteenth century anarchism was the creed of
many peasants in Valencia, Catalonia and Andalusia, where it had
strong millenarian overtones, as well as appealing to workers in the
cities. Anarcho-syndicalism dominated the early trade union movement. The national trade union confederation, the CNT, was from
its foundation in 1910 dominated by anarchists. During the Spanish
Civil War anarchism came briefly into its own. Spanish anarchism
revealed some very ugly and destructive tendencies—in the mass-
acres 'carried out by the Durutti column in Aragon or by the militia
in Madrid on their way to the front' (Gerald Brenan, *The Spanish
Labyrinth*, 318); and in the destruction of churches and works of
art. The anarchist movement also revealed its attractive and constructive possibilities. Peasants in parts of Castile and Aragon and in
Andalusia collectivized the land, and many of these villages launched
educational campaigns to end illiteracy, and tried to set up medical
services. They also adopted radical economic principles, often abolishing use of money. Catalonia was for a short time effectively controlled by the anarchists and from July to October 1936 there was
almost complete workers' control in the factories and public services
of Barcelona.

George Orwell, who went to Catalonia as a volunteer for the

International Brigade, recorded in *Homage to Catalonia* his first impressions of Barcelona :

> Practically every building of any size had been seized by the
> workers and was draped with red flags or with the red and black
> flag of the Anarchists ... Churches here and there were being
> systematically demolished by gangs of workmen. Every shop and
> café had an inscription saying that it had been collectivized ...
> Tipping was forbidden by law ... There were no private motor-cars,
> they had all been commandeered, and all the trams and taxis and
> much of the other transport were painted red and black ... Above
> all, there was a belief in the revolution and the future, a feeling
> of having suddenly emerged into an era of equality and freedom.
> Human beings were trying to behave as human beings and not as
> cogs in the capitalist machine. In the barbers' shops were Anarchist
> notices (the barbers were mostly Anarchists) solemnly explaining
> that barbers were no longer slaves. In the streets were coloured
> posters appealing to prostitutes to stop being prostitutes ... At
> that time revolutionary ballads of the naïvest kind ... were being
> sold on the streets for a few centimes each. I have often seen an
> illiterate militiaman buy one of these ballads, laboriously spell out
> the words, and then, when he had got the hang of it, begin singing
> it to an appropriate tune (8–10).

This experiment in running an anarchist society was ended when the anarchists were attacked by their allies, the Communists, and by the Republican Liberal Government, and was doomed even before the final victory of Franco's forces.

Anarchist ideas were transported across the Atlantic along with Italian, Russian, East European and German immigrants to the United States, and had some success in the comparatively weak labour movement of the 1880s and 1890s. The association between anarchism and acts of terrorism tended to discredit the movement in the 1900s. In the United 'States syndicalism is associated with the militant union the Industrial Workers of the World—the Wobblies—which was founded in 1905 and initially got its main support from the miners in the West. However anarchists were only one among several diverse influences in the IWW, where their stress on decentralism and federalism contrasted with Bill Haywood's aim of 'One Big Union' (see G. D. H. Cole, *A History of Socialist Thought*, Vol. III, Part 2).

But quite a different brand of anarchism had also taken root in America, and this native anarchism was, in accord with the American ethos, strongly individualist. Godwin's *Political Justice* was published in America in 1796; but a more formative influence on

later American anarchism was Josiah Warren's attempt to put individualist anarchism into practice, through experimental co-operatives, in the 1830s and 1840s. Warren propogated ideas on economic
organization and private property not unlike those Proudhon was
independently putting forward in France. Both influenced a later
exponent of individualist anarchism, Benjamin Tucker, whose major
contribution to the anarchist movement was as journalist and pub-
lisher. He brought out a translation of Max Stirner in 1907, and
Stirner's 'egoism' understood in American terms won some converts.
Tucker's belief in the need for individual non-co-operation with the
State, especially through tax refusal, linked him to another important figure in the American libertarian tradition, Henry David
Thoreau, who is remembered partly for his classic essay published
in 1840 *On the Duty of Civil Disobedience.* 'Under a government
which imprisons any unjustly', commented Thoreau, 'the true place
for a just man is also in prison' (see Peter Mayer, ed, *The Pacifist
Conscience,* 149).
    Tucker set out, however, to make anarchism respectable, as against
the violence advocated by European emigrés, and to combat all forms
of socialism and communism. In the economic sphere he attacked
monopolies, but deplored the 'all-inclusive monopoly' proposed by
the State socialists as an alternative. To replace monopolies he
appealed to the 'natural law of competition' and urged that laissez-
faire economics should be taken to its logical conclusion in totally
free trade, and an end to those restrictions which protect the privileges of capital. Many of Tucker's ideas have affinities with a certain
kind of conservatism, which opposes bureaucracy and 'collectivism'
in the name of individual liberty. As Bakunin saw, individualism,
which interprets liberty as the absence of social restrictions on the
individual, tends to be opposed to collective action to secure justice
and equality. Tucker was at the opposite pole from the syndicalists—
though he managed to avoid the conservative trap of preferring 'freedom' for economic trusts to any form of political control.
    Anarchism as a theoretical movement derives from European and
North American traditions, but it has had an important influence in
parts of the Third World, especially Latin America. Daniel Guérin in
his analytical survey *L'Anarchisme* stresses Bakunin's awareness of
the future importance of anti-colonial movements of national liberation, and his hope that these would also achieve social liberation of
the masses (81–2). Bakuninist ideas were introduced into Mexico,
Argentina and Cuba in the 1870s. Later in Mexico theoretical
anarchist influences merged with spontaneous peasant anarchism in
Zapata's campaign after 1910. Woodcock compares Zapata's movement with Makhno's attempt to create an anarchist society in the

Ukraine. Anarcho-syndicalist ideas stemming from Spain also influenced trade unions in many Latin American countries in the early years of this century. In the 1920s anarcho-syndicalism tended to give way before Communism, but has remained influential in Argentina.

In Asia anarchism spread to circles of students and intellectuals—to Japan 'where the small anarchist movement was completely destroyed after the execution of D. Kotoku and his comrades in January 1911' (Rudolph Rocker, *Anarcho-Syndicalism: Theory and Practice*, 200); to Indonesia under the impetus of the libertarian movement in Holland; to China where it was briefly revived after the Second World War; and to India. In India, however, a much more significant expression of near-anarchist ideas could be found in the Gandhian movement for national independence. Gandhi himself was influenced by both Tolstoy and Thoreau, but his philosophy was primarily a reinterpretation of elements in the Indian cultural tradition, and a response to immediate social and political conditions. So he cannot easily be fitted into Western political categories. The movement which has since Gandhi's death been led by Vinoba Bhave is village-based, anti-parliamentary and anti-governmental in its approach to land reform and social development. Its approach is in many senses anarchist, though the Gandhian movement itself is wary of accepting the anarchist label; and its avoidance of any direct resistance to the Indian Government would make many anarchists hesitant to identify with it (see Geoffrey Ostergaard, 'Indian Anarchism: The Sarvodaya Movement', *Government and Opposition*, 1970).

In the West anarchist movements with roots in the traditions of the last century are not now politically significant. There is, however, some evidence that in response to the political experience of the mid-twentieth century anarchism is being revived in more modern form in Western Europe and North America. The prevalence of anarchist and syndicalist ideas and organizational forms in the French student revolt of May 1968, and their partial spill-over into the factories, was one of the more dramatic illustrations that anarchist tendencies belong not only to the past but potentially to the future. Students in particular, turning away from both Western and official Socialist societies, are responsive to anarchism. Though their protests are a response to contemporary ills—the cold war, nuclear bombs, disillusionment with official politics—student rebellion does link up with traditional anarchism, as Paul Goodman stresses:

They believe in local power, community development, rural reconstruction, decentralist organization ... They prefer a simpler standard of living ... they do not trust the due process of

administrators and are quick to resort to direct action and civil
disobedience. All this adds up to the community Anarchism of
Kropotkin, the resistance Anarchism of Malatesta, the agitational
anarchism of Bakunin . . . (*Anarchy*, No. 96, February 1969, 47).

Anarchism is however only one strand in student unrest, and it is
still necessary to look for a modern formulation of anarchism primarily in the writings of their elders. Two of the main theorists
relevant here are Alex Comfort, whose career as a biologist, novelist
and poet encompasses writings on social psychology, sex and politics;
and Paul Goodman, the American novelist, poet and teacher whose
writings range from *gestalt* theory to town planning, and who is
directly influential among American students.

The nature of writings about anarchism may in part reflect the
background and experience of anarchist theorists. A great deal of
standard political theory has been written either by philosophers
(Plato—who was also a poet, but wished to suppress poetry in his
Republic; Hobbes, Locke, Hume, Hegel), or by those with experience
of government and state craft (Machiavelli, Burke, the Federalists,
De Tocqueville). Much anarchist thought has been elaborated by
individuals whose ideas emerged out of their activities in anti-
governmental movements—Bakunin, Malatesta, Emma Goldman for
example; a trait which anarchism shares with other utopian and
radical theories. Perhaps more interesting, much anarchist thought
has been elaborated by those whose commitments have been in the
sciences or the arts. Kropotkin was an eminent naturalist and geolo-
gist, committed to 'scientific method' in his social theory; and one of
the leading French anarchist propagandists at the end of the last
century, Elisée Reclus, was a well known geographer. Alex Comfort's
anarchist ideas are explicitly linked to both his scientific and his
artistic commitments (see, for instance, *Art and Social Responsibility*).

Paul Goodman comments on 'the humanistic and, so to speak,
ecological background of the anarchist leaders', noting that Fanelli
was an architect, Malatesta had studied medicine, and that 'Morris
was an arts and craftsman' (*People or Personnel*, 42). William Morris
can be linked to the general anarchist tradition because of his rebellion against industrialism, his opposition to parliamentary politics,
and the libertarian anti-governmental tone of his utopian picture in
News from Nowhere. On the other hand his organizational links
were with the English Marxist movement of the 1880s and 1890s,
and he explicitly disassociated himself from anarchism, remarking
that he had learned from some of his Anarchist friends 'quite against
their intention, that Anarchism was impossible (Asa Briggs, ed.,
William Morris: Selected Writings and Designs, 34–5). A number of

artists have been attracted towards anarchism. Shelley was a member of the Godwin circle, Gustave Courbet a friend of Proudhon, and Oscar Wilde an admirer of Kropotkin. Herbert Read, poet and art critic, became a leading exponent of anarchism in England in the 1930s and 1940s. In France around the turn of the century anarchism was adopted by Neo-Impressionist painters, notably the Pisarros (see *Anarchy*, No. 91, September 1968), and by Symbolist poets and writers. Among leading anarchists in Russia the poet Voline became a supporter of Makhno, and Tolstoy's pacifist and Christian style of anarchism emerged after he had written his major novels.

The social and cultural background of anarchist thinkers may be relevant both to understanding which social groups are attracted to anarchism, and the leading ideas and images in anarchist theory. The purpose of this book is not however to chart the development of the anarchist movement, nor to study in detail the theories of particular anarchist writers. It is rather to explore certain key themes and ideas within anarchism in relation to other traditions of political theory, and to contemporary political and social conditions.

It is not easy, as the very brief and incomplete sketch of the anarchist tradition given here indicates, to define the scope and limits of anarchism. In the following discussion both syndicalism and the Gandhian movement are treated as peripheral to the central development of anarchism. Not that they are unimportant—arguably both have more political relevance than a 'pure' anarchism, but they are not wholly accepted by anarchists as part of their tradition; and they both demand a more serious treatment than can be accorded them in the scope of this study.

1 The Political Theory of Anarchism

The Leviathan

This chapter examines some of the key concepts and themes of anarchism and their relation to orthodox political theory. The discussion centres round Hobbes's *Leviathan*. Because Hobbes stated with exceptional clarity and incisiveness some of the key problems of politics, and did so at a high level of abstraction which gives his philosophy a relatively timeless quality, it is possible to draw on his thought for the purposes of general analysis.

Hobbes is also particularly relevant to a discussion of anarchism. As a philosopher of rigorous 'realism' he contrasts strongly with the 'utopian' elements in anarchist thought; and the *Leviathan*, which is a classic statement of the need for strong government, persuasively equates anarchy with violence and disorder. But interestingly Godwin, the first philosopher of anarchism, is in the direct line of intellectual descent from Hobbes's individualism and rationalism. It is, therefore, possible to point to the complexity of political ideas, by tracing how Hobbes's theory can generate its own opposite—a consistent individualist anarchist theory, whilst at the same time laying the theoretical foundations for an anarchist inversion of itself.

Anarchist ideas can be linked with Hobbes's theory at three levels. First, at the most obvious level, an anarchist vision of a peaceful society free from the ills of government, is a reverse image of Hobbes's picture of the state of war which results when government breaks down, or in the absence of any central power. Secondly, there are interesting connections to be made between Hobbes's psychology and conception of the individual, and anarchist attitudes. Thirdly, Hobbesian propositions about the state, the role of law, and the nature of crime, illuminate the central concerns of anarchism. There are limitations in the Hobbesian account of society which takes the psychological make-up of the individual as the basis for analysis, and self-interest—even the enlightened self interest leading to virtuous behaviour Godwin envisages—as the motive force holding society together. But the emphasis of many later anarchists on the positive role of social groups in influencing and binding together individuals provides a partial solution for some of the difficulties inherent in this position.

Anarchy means literally 'without government', and the lowest common denominator of anarchist thought is the conviction that existing forms of government are productive of wars, internal violence, repression and misery. This critique of government extends to liberal democratic governments as well as to the more frequently criticized dictatorships. Hobbes was, like the anarchists, more interested in government as a general phenomenon than in distinguishing between different types of government. While he thought monarchial government would be more efficient and less open to corruption than other forms, he was primarily concerned to explain in abstract terms why government is necessary.

The Social Contract

Hobbes's abstract justification for government rests on the legalistic fiction of the social contract. The contract is envisaged between individuals driven to set up a government because of the miseries they endure in the 'state of nature', where there is no stable social organization. The state of nature is sometimes envisaged in a quasi-historical way : once upon a time, before government existed, men lived in small scattered groups—sometimes perhaps joined together in bands for hunting or war—and tried to live off the land. But no one could cultivate the land in peace, or be secure in his possessions, because at any time he might be attacked by marauders and driven off or killed. Therefore, everyone had to be ready to fight off attackers; and men were likely to attack both for the sake of possessions and the power which possessions bring; or through sheer love of fighting and the glory to be won from success in battle. Even if only a minority were likely to act in this fashion, everyone was forced through fear to take defensive measures, and might, in line with the familiar logic of defence, feel impelled to launch preventive attacks against their more threatening neighbours.

Hobbes is not claiming to describe an actual historical situation—even though in the seventeenth century historical and anthropological evidence would not have thrown as much doubt as they do now on the realism of his picture of a pre-social stage. He is exploring the logic of a situation in which human nature predisposes men to act in certain ways, and there is no superior power to prevent them warring with one another. So in the state of nature there is no economic prosperity—because economic advance depends on security and co-operation; no scientific knowledge, 'no arts; no letters; no society; and which is worst of all, continual fear and danger of violent death' (*Leviathan*, 82). This is an extreme picture of what life would be like without any government at all. Superimposed on this are images of a partial 'state of nature' resulting from the breakdown of central government, or civil war—the realistic dangers Hobbes is trying to avert.

Hobbes is aware that the state of nature in which there is no organized society is a logical fiction; it is the basis for the second fiction, the social contract. Individuals who have been driven by fear and guided by reason to seek a rational solution to their difficulties are envisaged as coming together to draw up what amounts to a peace treaty, and simultaneously setting up a sovereign to ensure the treaty is in future kept. The articles of the treaty, and the obligations of the parties to it, are spelt out in full on the analogy of other legally binding contracts, for example in the commercial sphere. Hobbes is able through this analogy to argue a double case. First, he shows that it is in the interest of the individual to live under strong government, and therefore he should act in such a way as to maintain the existing government (i.e. keep the terms of the 'social contract'). Secondly, by drawing on the sophisticated concepts and sense of moral obligation evolved in legal practice and familiar to his readers, Hobbes is able to suggest why government is not only necessary and useful, but has legitimate authority.

Hobbes is the most brilliant and original of the contract theorists, but the conception of the social contract is common to many other seventeenth century writers. It was carried over into the eighteenth century, but by the time of the French Revolution it had lost much of its orginal relevance as a political analogy; and it had also lost its logical clarity as a result of being merged in political discourse with the Whig interpretation of British history, and being identified with the settlement of 1688. Moreover, by this time contract theory often seemed designed to justify existing political practices, which struck many reformers and radicals as corrupt, unjust and frequently absurd. As a result the contract tended to look like a form of intellectual mystification, designed to delude the people into foregoing their rights. The theoretical foundations of the contract theory were undermined by Hume. Bentham attacked the fiction of the contract in the name of utilitarianism; Tom Paine derided, in defence of popular sovereignty, the idea of a contract which vested in the Government continuing rights; and William Godwin dismissed the notion of an 'original contract' in the course of constructing a rational anarchist philosophy.

But the idea of the contract did not simply disappear; as is frequent with political conceptions, it underwent a series of transformations. The notion of individual consent to government, which is intrinsic to the social contract, has inherently radical implications, as Hobbes was uneasily aware; and as Locke carefully demonstrated in his defence of rebellion. These radical possibilities were developed in three directions. The utilitarian theory of democracy retained the implicit contractual notions of utility as a criterion of the purpose of government, and of individual consent, as a criterion of legitimacy, whilst abandoning the legal fiction of the contract. In the radical democratic theory propagated by Paine the historical fiction was transmuted into a present and recurring renewal of the contract between the governed and their chosen government; and sovereignty was transferred from the 'sovereign' monarch to the people. The anarchist conception developed by Godwin went a stage further than Paine. Godwin thought of contracts not between that fictitious entity, the 'people', and the government; but between specific individuals. Whereas Hobbes's society is based on a single compact in the assumed past, Godwin's society is to be built on a series of mutual and constantly renewed compacts between freely contracting individuals; permanent contracts like marriage are an infringement of freedom. This conception of contracts based on the principle of justice implicit in Godwin, was built systematically into the social theory of Proudhon, who contrasted voluntary contract with law enforced by superior power.

The impact of Hobbes's theory lies partly in the image he evokes of the violence, chaos and fear which ensue when there is no government to enforce law and order. If his assumptions are reversed, and one argues that men are by nature—when uncorrupted by the perverting influence of government and evil societies—co-operative, peace-loving and activated by spontaneous sympathy towards others, then the logic of the situation is also reversed. Government ceases to be a protector of individuals, and a guarantor of their lives and property. Instead, the State is seen as the chief threat to the liberty, security and prosperity of the individual, whom it circumscribes with laws and regulations, jails for infringement of these rules, conscripts to fight in wars, executes for any treason to the state, and robs through exorbitant taxes. Hobbes conceded that governments might harm their subjects, but argued the worst a government could do to people is 'scarce sensible in respect of the miseries, and horrible calamities, that accompany a civil war, or that dissolute condition of masterless men, without subjection to laws, and a coercive power to tie their hands from rapine and revenge (*Leviathan*, 120). Anarchists like Godwin and Tolstoy believed that governments are responsible for the greatest crimes, and promote devastating wars between states. It is of course an over-simplification to say that anarchists believe men are always naturally co-operative and peaceable, just as it is misleading to suggest Hobbes thought all men are necessarily competitive and vainglorious. But Hobbes's emphasis led him to the conclusion that government is a necessary evil. The anarchists conclude that government is a great and unnecessary evil, and that anarchy in the literal sense of no government need not mean anarchy in the popular sense of violence and disorder.

Hobbes and Godwin

But apart from the basic image of Hobbes's state of nature in reverse, there are more direct and subtle links between Hobbes and one strand of the anarchist tradition—that is the individualist and rationalist tradition represented especially by William Godwin. Hobbes's theory contains the ingredients of a consistent theory of anarchism, and these are present in Godwin's writings. The most basic element common to both is the theoretical framework—the assumption that social analysis starts with the individual, and his personal needs and desires, rather than with society, the state, or the pattern of history. Godwin considers it obvious that 'society is nothing more than an aggregate of individuals'. The individual is for purposes of analysis abstracted from society. The importance of education into society is recognized by Hobbes, and even more so by Godwin; but political conclusions are based on deductions from human nature, which is seen as more fundamental than any specific social or cultural influence. Stemming from this individualist position are Hobbes's and Godwin's views on freedom, equality, rationality, and the nature of the state.

Hobbes defines freedom as the absence of external constraints on the individual. The underlying assumption is that freedom to do what one likes is for the individual a fundamental good, and though some social restraints may be necessary for the sake of peace, they are inevitably irksome to the individual. Once Hobbes's overriding emphasis on strong government in the interests of preventing civil disorder has been replaced by a more sanguine reliance on a natural harmony of interests—for example, through the mechanism of the market—then the logical consequence is laissez-faire liberalism, in which there is a residual Hobbesian belief in the role of the state in maintaining internal peace and providing defence against external enemies, but the restrictive sphere of the state is reduced to a minimum. If this brand of liberalism is taken to its logical extreme, what results is a kind of laissez-faire anarchism postulating a natural harmony of individual interests in all spheres of social life.

Hobbes not only creates a conception of individual freedom ultimately subversive of his own belief in the overriding rights of govern-

ment; he also espouses a radical egalitarianism. There are three
reasons for his emphasis on the basic equality of all men. One is the
specific political desire to deny to the nobility a priviliged, and hence
disruptive, status in the realm: all men are equally obliged to obey
the sovereign. Secondly, the basic equality of men in the state of
nature is a necessary postulate if all men are to have an equal incentive to live under a sovereign. If in a state of nature some men
through superior strength or intelligence could secure permanent
power and security, then the logic of the situation would dictate
their remaining in a state of anarchy. Hobbes does not argue what is
obviously untrue, that men all have exactly the same degree of
strength or same degree of intelligence, but that these inherent
differences are not significant, since men continuously compete with
one another. Above all, men are equal in their vulnerability to violent
death. This vulnerability is more significant than accidental personal
attributes or artificial social trappings. Here Hobbes takes up his
third and most radical argument for equality. He refuses to accept
that it is part of the order of the universe (or ordained by God)
that some sections of humanity are 'naturally' superior to others;
the aristocracy are not superior by nature, but by social convention; and women are not inferior by nature, but by family
convention.

Hobbes is undermining with his critical rationality the social traditions of aristocracy and of the patriarchal family. As Burke later saw
when trying to maintain the values of tradition—and appealing to
the God-given order of the universe which enshrines the traditional
order of society—abstract and critical reasoning in politics is inherently radical, in the sense of destroying the previously unquestioned beliefs and habits of thought which maintain and shelter
social institutions. Once egalitarianism has been posited, in however
abstract terms, then the way is open for pursuing the logic of ideas
to more radical political conclusions. Godwin takes up the concept of
equality. He too accepts that men are not identical in their physical
or mental powers. But he argues in his *Enquiry Concerning Political
Justice*: 'There is no such disparity among the human race, as to
enable one man to hold several other men in subjection, except so far
as they are willing to be subject' (Vol. I, 145). More importantly, all
men and women are morally equal. Therefore, justice demands they
should be socially and economically equal.

The role of rationality in Hobbes's philosophy is complex. In his
psychology Hobbes stresses that rationality is the servant of the
passions: 'For the thoughts are to the desires, as scouts, and spies, to
range abroad, and find the way to the things desired' (*Leviathan*, 46).
Even when men decide to leave the state of nature, fear is the spur.

On the other hand, man's reason is a crucial bridge between the state of nature and civil society—the contract assumes both a sophisticated rational awareness of what is necessary, and the temporary dominance of a rational sense of long term self-interest. This excessive reliance on reason in the formation of the social contract stems from the exigencies of the contract fiction, and is dropped when Hobbes comes to consider how far men can be relied on to keep the contract. However, Hobbes's position is further complicated by the rationalist method and commitment of the *Leviathan*. Its brilliance and persuasive power is partly due to Hobbes's method of rigorously logical deduction from a priori principles on the model of his admired geometry. Hobbes himself is committed to belief in the power of reason in the development of science: both natural and social science.

Faith in the power of science entails a belief in the key role of reason in man's control over his natural and social environment, and is associated with the theory of progress, and with the optimism which characterized the rationalist temper of the Enlightenment. Godwin puts his trust in reason as the basis for a civilized society, and as the guarantor of progress towards a better one. But whilst Hobbes presumed reason can show us how to create a stable society through political science, but cannot guide political life, Godwin relies on reason to direct the passions continuously, and to prescribe day to day rules of behaviour in accordance with the principles of justice. Reason—which in Godwin has taken on Platonic overtones totally absent from Hobbes—will be the basis for contracts between free and mutually assenting individuals.

The method of *Political Justice* is also similar to that of the *Leviathan*. Godwin himself defined it in a preface to *The Enquirer* as a process of a priori reasoning by 'laying down one or two simple principles which seem scarcely to be exposed to the hazard of refutation, and then developing them, applying them to a number of points, and following them into a variety of inferences', so constructing a total system which should 'overbear and annihilate all opposition' (H. S. Salt, ed., *Political Justice*, 12).

It follows from both the individualism and rationalism of the Hobbesian kind of approach that the state is seen as primarily a coercive organization. The state exists to serve the interests of individuals, and to maintain law and order among unruly individuals it requires the use of force. The sovereign enforces the social contract to maintain the security of the commonwealth; for 'covenants without the sword are but words, and of no strength to secure a man at all' (*Leviathan*, 109). The anarchists agree that the state is distinguished above all by its coercive power. This means that government 'even in its best state is an evil' for Godwin. Later anarchists have stressed this point with greater passion. For Tolstoy the guillotine has superseded the sword as the symbol of government. For Emma Goldman the machinery of government comprises 'the club, the gun, the handcuff, or the prison' (*Anarchism and Other Essays*, 54).

Primacy of the Individual

At this point I wish to drop the detailed comparison between Hobbes and Godwin and to take up some more tenuous but interesting links between Hobbes and various strands of the anarchist tradition. Earlier in the discussion it was indicated that the Hobbesian assertion of the primacy of the individual is at least potentially subversive of the state. Hobbes is prepared to subordinate the interests of the individual to state power, but only for strictly limited and practical reasons—to increase general security. Hobbes is not prepared to sacrifice individual interests to any social grouping, to any political cause, moral ideal or religious faith. The Great Leviathan is never in any sense sacred. Hobbes does not appeal to the divinity of kings. Nor does he make any of the modern appeals to the idea of the nation, the motherland, the cause, or the just war. Indeed any kind of unconditional loyalty or fanatical devotion are alien to Hobbes. If the government is losing its grip, then the individual is encouraged to use his common sense and to look after himself.

Hobbes is opposing two kinds of loyalty and idealism : an aristocratic and heroic code of honour which because it is heroic is also very destructive of peace and quiet; and religious or political idealism and devotion to a cause, a more contemporary phenomenon. The first attitude was represented by the Royalists; the second by the Puritans and the Parliamentarians in the Civil War. Hobbes's critique of misguided enthusiasm is based on a strong sense of the political necessity of order. But it is also based on an assumption that fear is a natural—and therefore healthy and sensible—emotion. Hobbes used to joke about his own timid disposition. In his own words, at the outbreak of the Civil War, he was 'the first of all that fled'. When Cromwell had won, Hobbes was one of the first Royalists to make his peace with the new government. This prudential concern for one's own safety takes in Hobbes the form of political obedience to any strong government, and imposes a political obligation to maintain this obedience unless the government ceases to be effective.

But if this attitude is extended, as it was for example by Hobbes's

contemporary Anthony Ascham, who wrote a treatise on *The Confusions and Revolutions of Government*, then it may become a totally
apolitical position, if not an anti-political one. Ascham addressed
himself to the mass of ordinary people: 'the Anvill on which all
sorts of Hammers discharge themselves' (see Irene Coltman, *Private
Men and Public Causes*, 199). All politics becomes in this view a
dangerous and troublesome interruption of day to day life. And this
personal day to day life is all that matters to the individual. So if
contending politicians start fighting over one's territory, then one
protects oneself as best one can, and co-operates with whoever is
winning at a particular time. This attitude makes connections with
a popular revolt against the heroism and ambitions of the upper
classes; and with elements in the intellectual anarchist tradition—
the appeal to the commonsense and natural instincts of the man in the
street against the inflated claims of the state, and the propaganda
and ritual of war. The insistence that the individual's first good is his
own can be converted back into a subversive kind of 'politics'. Alex
Comfort in a review of Herbert Marcuse salutes the idea that 'pig-
politics is to be overthrown, not by a revolutionary clique or an
irrational mob, but by the weapon of "Irish democracy"—the withdrawal, resistance and ennui of the ordinary person—in other words
by rational, dogged human bloodymindedness' (*The Guardian*, 22
May, 1969, 9).

Hobbes's detailed psychological theory links up with another
anarchist attitude—a libertarian approach to the pleasures of life,
and, in particular, sex. Hobbes takes the importance of men's desires
and passions for granted, and avoids any condemnation of them.
There is no hierarchy of higher and lower passions; no puritanism or
asceticism. Man is a kind of machine propelled onward by a succession of desires. This view, which has its inherent limitations—
viz. Bentham's famous 'quantity of pleasure being equal, pushpin
is as good as poetry'—is subversive both of social taboos and of a
social morality which demands suppression and punishment of
vice.

Belief in the naturalness of men's desires can be developed into a
positive plea to encourage individuals to satisfy their desires and
find happiness. The French utopian socialist Charles Fourier constructed a picture of a community which would ensure harmony
through giving scope to different human passions. Instead of suppressing and perverting these desires, as he believed early nineteenth
century society did, Fourier's communities would provide creative
outlets for them in the form of useful work and in free personal
relationships. In spite of eccentricities of detail, Fourier's psychological
approach has connexions with modern libertarian attitudes. These

attitudes have however been greatly influenced by the psychology of Freud, especially as developed by neo-Freudians who have questioned Freud's own pessimistic conclusions. Social and even political evils may in this view be traced to the harmful repression of natural drives—the word 'repression' taking on a double significance. This approach involves rejection of traditional institutions, conventional moral codes, and religious conceptions of sin. In its iconoclasm, though not in its tone, modern libertarianism still has certain connexions with Hobbesian scepticism.

Law and Government

A more direct agreement between Hobbes and anarchist thinkers is in their view of law. Hobbes is one of those theorists who defines law purely as the will of the sovereign. The authority of the law stems from the fact that the sovereign has willed it, not because it corresponds to the laws of nature or principles of natural justice. If the legitimacy of the sovereign's authority is denied, so the legitimacy of the law; and if one believes in independent standards of justice and morality—as anarchists do—existing laws may be judged morally unjust. Moreover, if government itself is an evil, then the laws promulgated by governments are not only coercive restrictions on individual liberty—which Hobbes would accept, but an intolerable form of coercion.

An individualist critique of the intrinsic evil of coercive law is usually backed by another anarchist argument: that laws are largely designed to protect property, and therefore are a bastion for the privileges of wealth. Proudhon summed up the idea that the laws protecting property are a form of injustice in his celebrated slogan 'Property is Theft'. This conception had already been put forward forcibly by Godwin:

> The fruitful source of crimes consists in this circumstance, one
> man's possessing in abundance that of which another man is
> destitute . . . Accumulated property has fixed its empire (H. S. Salt,
> ed., *Political Justice*, 58–9).

If the existing laws are unjust, then breaking the law may be a natural if unwise response to injustice (as Godwin saw it), or a quite legitimate form of rebellion, as some later anarchists, who often tended to romanticize criminals, claimed. An intellectualized view of the criminal as a rebel against an unjust and repressive society gains some colour and depth from the folk traditions in which common people have sometimes respected robbers and bandits as heroic protectors and avengers of the poor.

A second element in the anarchist opposition to laws, and the law courts, police forces, and prisons which enforce them, is the conviction that the evils stemming from judicial and punitive institutions are far greater than the results of occasional crime. This belief is partly a response to the suffering of men and women sent to jail. Emma Goldman wrote in an essay on 'Prisons':

> There is not a single penal institution or reformatory in the
> United States where men are not tortured 'to be made good', by
> means of the black-jack, the club, the strait-jacket, the water-cure,
> the 'humming bird' (an electrical contrivance run along the human
> body), the solitary, the bull-ring, and starvation diet ... But
> prison walls rarely allow the agonized shrieks of the victims to
> escape—prison walls are thick, they dull the sound (*Anarchism
> and Other Essays*, 83–4).

The related anarchist argument—that prisons increase crime—Emma Goldman illustrates from Oscar Wilde's *Ballad of Reading Gaol*:

> The vilest deeds, like poison weeds,
> Bloom well in prison air;
> It is only what is good in Man
> That wastes and withers there.

The third argument here, which is more original to anarchists, is that the whole system of law enforcement creates 'criminals' among those who enforce the law. Kropotkin commented on 'the torrent of depravity let loose in human society by the "informing" which is countenanced by judges, and paid in hard cash by governments', and the corruption entailed in a system which demands men become executioners and jailers (*Law and Authority*, 22–3). Wilde observed in *The Soul of Man under Socialism* that in reading history one is sickened 'not by the crimes that the wicked have committed, but by the punishments that the good have inflicted' which are in fact far more brutalizing for the community (36).

This type of analysis can be extended to a more central attack on the uses and abuses of power to encompass government as a whole. It may be argued that competition for power and position in government encourages those personalities seeking dominance and prestige, so the vast power and responsibility inherent in government may be put in the hands of those intrinsically least fitted for this role. Secondly, even if initially men go into politics with a sense of social responsibility, the nature of the political system and the means necessary to achieve one's goals may over time corrupt political practitioners. A further refinement of this analysis rests on an examination of the role of bureaucracy in eroding any sense of direct responsibility for governmental or judicial actions, by creating an immense psychological distance between those who make decisions and those who carry out orders—between the head of State and the soldier in the field, between the judge and the hangman. This anarchist concern has been expressed most insistently by contemporary anarchist writers faced with the phenomena of twentieth century technology and the enormous extension of State bureaucracy. Paul Goodman recognizes the scope of the problem in a pamphlet on *Drawing The Line*. He quotes from a sergeant writing about a bombed area in Germany:

> In modern war there are crimes not criminals ... Here, as in many cases, the guilt belonged to the machine. Somewhere in the apparatus of bureaucracy, memoranda, and clean efficient directives, a crime has been committed (5).

Goodman goes on to attack this approach and to argue that individual responsibility must be accepted:

> For every one knows moments in which he conforms against his nature, in which he suppresses his best spontaneous impulse, and cowardly takes leave of his heart (5–6).

The behaviour which continues to make war crimes possible can be imputed; why is the sergeant still a sergeant?

Examining the impact of bureaucracy is an exercise in sociological analysis and therefore enters into a realm outside the concerns of Hobbesian, or indeed Godwinian, political theory, which makes its deductions on the basis of purely individual psychology. The limitations of the individualist social theory stemming from Hobbes are the limitations of Hobbes himself. What is missing is the necessary dependence of the individual on a wider social group, and the understanding that a developed sense of individuality is in itself a social product. The Hobbesian conception of freedom as the absence of external restraints on the individual would only be possible in a society with a highly developed sense of individuality and allowing a considerable degree of personal freedom.

Society and the Individual

The missing dimension of 'society' suggests a possible solution to the Hobbesian dilemma of either anarchic competitive individuals or else a coercive Leviathan to keep them in order. Society may create the kind of individuals who have strongly internalized values and can live co-operatively and freely without the threat of force. Secondly, the term 'society' suggests that people already live in some kind of social unit, so social organization is not just imposed artificially by contract and maintained by force. Instead there may be 'natural' social units already existing and maintaining an unforced co-operation.

This solution of looking to 'society' was in fact seized on by some anarchists, for instance Kropotkin. Darwin's theory of evolution had resulted in a revival of Hobbesian social theory stressing individualism and the role of competition. To combat this Kropotkin drew on anthropology and history to show that closely knit communities antedate individual competition. In this nineteenth century sense society is usually opposed to the State. In Hobbes 'society', in so far as the concept enters into his picture at all, is defined by the State. But for anarchists and many socialists, society becomes the opposite of the State. Society is the repository of all the good aspects of social life and organization—co-operation, sympathy, affection, initiative and spontaneity. While the State incorporates all the bad aspects of social interaction—coercion, force and domination; and politics tends to be seen as the arena of force, fraud and trickery. The State is an incubus upon society—a distorting factor.

But there are problems in turning to society. The concept of society in itself is empty, and it may be made the repository of differing sets of ideas or differing images. Conservative theorists, like Burke, can draw on society as a product of national history and tradition to defend the existing state and social order. Or utopian thinkers can draw up pictures of social conditioning in an ideal society which is too narrowly and rigidly defined to allow for a truly anarchist freedom of individualism. Moreover, actual societies, far from filling the bill, may be said to actively foster competition and aggression, or to promote attitudes which support the existing State; while present social institutions and groupings may subordinate the individual further to the State rather than provide the basis for an alternative social order. So 'society' is the answer to the key problem of how to achieve organized co-operation among individuals—beyond the level of small groups—without resorting to coercion and the sanctions of force, largely at an ideal and abstract level. Nevertheless it provides an important theoretical advance on the Godwin model of political analysis, and may provide an advance in practice if the anarchist society is seen as a goal to work towards—i.e. if linked to social activism.

For one limitation in a theoretical approach based on individual self-interest is that in its immediate political application it tends either toward passive obedience—as it is meant to in Hobbes; or in anarchist versions towards passive disobedience and a purely personal opting out, which is not likely to further the anarchist aims of preventing injustice or changing society. In Godwin there is the more constructive alternative of social change through persuasion and education. But a method which relies on influencing individuals not only involves a perhaps excessive faith in reason, but ignores the sociological significance of institutions and the political importance of power.

Activism in the anarchist tradition has often been associated with the individual heroic gesture of 'propaganda by deed', or assassination, which Lenin dubbed contemptuously, in *What Is To Be Done*, as the 'spontaneity' of the intellectuals, and criticized for its political irrelevance. Many anarchists were unhappy about the image of anarchism which acts of terrorism propagated, and the tendency for this method sometimes to rebound in assassination attempts against some of the leading anarchists. Some, like Tolstoy, objected to violence in principle, and others, like Kropotkin, gave support largely out of loyalty to anarchist comrades.

Other anarchists did not object to violence as such but adopted a more Marxist position, that the only effective violence was the combined and organized force of the working class. Malatesta was spokesman for this view. Organization is necessarily crucial for any movement relying on mass action, and trying to build up support among workers in the teeth of opposition and repression by employers and police. Joe Hill, song writer for the Wobblies, on the eve of his execution for murder in 1915 (it was widely believed he was framed) sent an appropriate farewell telegram urging 'Don't waste time mourning, organize'. But for anarchists the necessity of organization, and the demands of a general strategy for a movement, both seem in danger of undermining the anarchists' own ideals. Problems of organization within the revolutionary movement are also central to the disagreements between anarchists and socialists.

The importance of organization bears on the other key disagreement between anarchists and socialists—the role of government after a socialist revolution. Socialists have not in general the same intrinsic distrust of government which characterizes anarchists, and many socialists accept the concept of popular sovereignty within the radical democratic tradition espoused by Paine. Anarchists retain a deep distrust of 'democratic' governments. Proudhon argued in 1848 that universal suffrage was a form of counter-revolution; and his slogan that democracy is a form of dictatorship was being repeated by students in Paris in May 1968. For anarchists the legalistic trappings of elections or plebiscites—the 'mandate' and the expression of the 'will of the people'—are as fictitious as the 'original social contract', and have, like the contract concept, been adapted to the uses of political propaganda. Indeed, in the name of popular sovereignty the government may arrogate to itself powers not dreamed of in Hobbes's philosophy.

2   Anarchism and the State

State and Government

Opposition to the State is central to anarchism. But what is meant by the State in political theorizing is frequently ambiguous, partly because there are substantive theoretical issues at stake. Some attempt at definition must, however, be made, and there are two distinctions which have considerable importance. These are the distinction between State and Government—though many anarchists have used the words interchangeably; and the distinction between State and Society—which is now commonly reflected in our thought and language.

The State is usually associated with its main organs—the administrative bureaucracy, the police and the army; from an anarchist viewpoint the judiciary and the Church may also be seen as adjuncts of State power. The main anarchist analysis of the State was formullated in the nineteenth century. Nicolas Walter recently commented in the journal *Anarchy*:

> The anarchist literature of the past weighs heavily on the present,
> and makes it hard for us to produce a new literature for the
> future. And yet, though the works of our predecessors are
> numerous, most of them are out of print, and the rest are mostly
> out of date (No. 100, June 1969, 161).

Contemporary anarchist writing does not deal in detail with the nature of political power or the modern State; and where it does discuss these questions the emphasis is primarily psychological. In his anthology on anarchism, Irving Louis Horowitz, after locating bureaucracy as an issue central to anarchism, has to fall back on a non-anarchist sociologist for a contemporary examination of this phenomenon. But recent political trends are important to an understanding of a renewed interest in anarchism, and in assessing the current validity of anarchist principles: so some attempt is made in this chapter to relate anarchist ideas to modern realities.

In its critique of the State anarchism has parallels with the tradition of liberal constitutionalism, which is associated in the eighteenth century with Whig theory in England and with Montesquieu in France, and evolved into one strand of nineteenth century liberalism.

Constitutionalism also shares with anarchism a deep distrust of democratic government and democratic ideology when conjoined to State
power; this link is very clear in the work of the contemporary French
theorist Bertrand De Jouvenel, who draws on the writings of Proudhon. One of the greatest writers in the constitutionalist tradition,
De Tocqueville, tried to adapt its leading ideas to conform with the
new democratic spirit, and his resultant emphasis on the value of
decentralism and voluntary association brings him at some levels
close to Kropotkin.

A useful starting point for discussion of the State is Kropotkin's
attempt to dispel confusion about terminology. Kropotkin remarks
in his pamphlet on *The State* that :

> State and government represent two ideas of a different kind. The
> State not only includes the existence of a power placed above
> society, but also a *territorial concentration and a concentration of
> many or even all functions of the life of society in the hands of a
> few* (10).

Kropotkin argues that to understand the State one must understand
its historical origins and development; this historical analysis also
reveals how the State differs from Society. 'Men have lived in societies
for thousands of years before having known the State.' For European nations the State 'hardly dates from the sixteenth century'.
Kropotkin suggests that the Roman Empire had all the characteristics
of a State, and that the images of law and sovereignty derived from
Rome, which influenced the bureaucratic and legal evolution of the
new European States, have dominated the attitudes of lawyers and
theorists ever since. What makes the State is 'the Triple Alliance,
constituted at last, of the military chief, the Roman judge, and the
priest, forming a mutual insurance for domination' (25). In the
modern State these roles are extended, but for anarchists its salient
characteristics remain an organized use of force to compel obedience,
a system of penal laws and administrative codes operated by experts,
and a set of beliefs and ceremonies which enshrine the State power
in the hearts of its subjects. Kropotkin's analysis is close to that of
the sociologist Max Weber, who defined the modern State in terms
of jurisdiction over a specific territorial area, a bureaucratic administration, and a monopoly of legitimate force within its borders.

In an early work on *Anarchism* the German jurist, Paul Eltzbacher, defined the State as 'a legal relation by virtue of which a
supreme authority exists in a certain territory' (18). The fact that it is
a legal relationship excludes for Eltzbacher purely arbitrary domination through conquest (a conquered country is perhaps a colony, but
not a State) and also an anarchist utopia governed only by moral

laws. The role of territorial boundaries means that neither a Church, whose membership is defined by faith, nor a nomadic tribe, in which membership is defined by kinship, are States, though both may have forms of government. Eltzbacher assumes in his juristic definition what Kropotkin emphasizes in a sociological and historical approach —that a State implies a territory of a certain size and a concentration of power. Hence the ancient cities of Greece, or medieval city republics, were not States in Kropotkin's sense. The historical phenomenon we now identify as the State is primarily represented in the European tradition by the national kingdoms which emerged out of the plurality of the Middle Ages.

The Evolution of the State

In the Middle Ages some monarchies did indeed have their national territories and made claims to sovereign power within them. But these monarchies were part of European Christendom, their subjects members of the Catholic Church; and the monarchs themselves were bound by religious allegiance to respect edicts from Rome, and politically restricted by the countervailing claims of the Pope to establish the rule of a Universal Church. Moreover, the Church claimed independent jurisdiction over its own affairs within the territorial realm of the King. As Ernest Barker stresses in a lecture on the State, the clergy were only one of the three medieval Estates limiting the King's powers. The second comprised the feudal nobles, 'who individually acted as sovereigns, so far as they could, in their local fiefs, and collectively formed a baronage ready to dispute authority at the centre as a body of rival kings' (*Principles of Social and Political Theory*, 13). Thirdly there were the 'commons', who 'locally sought autonomy for their municipal governments and their various merchant and craft gilds, and centrally, if they were joined together in an assembly of "the Commons" might join the baronage in challenging the king'. Barker concludes that 'there was little of a national State—indeed there was little of any sort of State—in the territorial *regnum* of the Middle Ages. It was a paradise of Estates rather than the pattern of a State' (12). Bertrand De Jouvenel in his book on *Power*, which he identifies with State power, attacks the misconception that monarchy could claim a divine absolutism in the Middle Ages. We should remember that:

> Power in medieval times was shared . . . limited (by other
> authorities which were, in their own sphere, autonomous), and
> that, above all, it was not sovereign (35).

Far from being sovereign in the sense of being absolute and above
the law, Power was 'tied down, not only in theory but in practice,
by the *Lex Terrae* (the customs of the country), which was thought
of as a thing immutable' (35).

The gradual emergence of a territorial state in which the government could claim sovereign power within its borders is closely related
to the development of a standing army. The existence of a permanent
army simultaneously increased the demands made by governments
on their subjects, especially in the realm of taxation, and their power
to quell rebellion against these demands. External wars might also
be used by monarchs to keep their subjects quiet at home. Hobbes
comments that:

> kings and persons of sovereign authority, because of their inde-
> pendency, are in continual jealousies, and in the state and posture
> of gladiators; having . . . their forts, garrisons and guns on the
> frontiers of their kingdoms; . . . But because they uphold thereby,
> the industry of their subjects; there does not follow from it, that
> misery, which accompanies the liberty of particular men (*Levia-
> than*, 83).

Hobbes's *Leviathan* can indeed be seen as one of the clearest statements of the new Absolutism, in which the sovereign power is not
hindered by any rival bodies in the State, the sovereign's will is above
the law (which it creates) and the sovereign rules within his territory
through his command of organized force. Hobbes explains that the
only way the participants in the social contract can erect a common
power to defend them is:

> to confer all their power and strength upon one man, or upon one
> assembly of men, that may reduce all their wills, by plurality of
> voices, unto one will . . . (112).

In this way Hobbes sees the multitude being united in one 'person',
who combines the power of all individuals under the direction of a
unifying will to create 'that great LEVIATHAN, or rather to speak
more reverently of that *mortal god*, to which we owe under the
immortal God our peace and defence'.

Hobbes would very much prefer that the 'sovereign' who 'represents' the State both at home as author of all government acts, and
abroad as head of State, should be a monarch, upon whom all the
attributes of sovereignty coalesce. This conception was summed up
by the *Roi Soleil* when he said 'L'etat, c'est moi.' But Hobbes insisted
that logically his theory applied equally to a governing assembly,
who could claim to represent and so embody the wills of the people.
This point is important, as De Jouvenel brings out. Other theorists

more or less contemporary with Hobbes were claiming that the King's right to rule derived from divine authority. But Hobbes made the real source of authority the people. The sovereign monarch is at the same time the representative of the people; his will represents their wills, and the absoluteness of his power stems from this delegation of authority. When, as in the French Revolution, the 'people' or the 'nation' claim their sovereignty and overthrow the tyranny of princes, then they elect a popular assembly to represent their will— the concepts of the Revolutionaries derived in part from Hobbes via Rousseau. But a government ruling through the 'will of the people', and so bound neither by belief in the eternal laws of God, nor by the previous customary laws of the country, may become the most arbitrary despotism, against which there is no appeal. And the people may discover that they are no better off than before, indeed they may be worse off. De Jouvenel comments:

> How very strange! When their masters were kings, the peoples never stopped complaining at having to pay war taxes. Then, when they have overthrown these masters and taken to taxing themselves, the currency in which they pay is not merely a part of their incomes but their very lives! (*Power*, 20).

If the despotism inherent in the unitary and secular State can sometimes be seen even more clearly in an era of 'democracy' than kingship, so also can the outlines of State power. It is probably only in a period of democratic aspiration and overthrow of governments that the idea of a 'state machinery' separate from government could take shape. Whilst earlier kings, as Kropotkin stresses, had their own growing bureaucracies, and their armies and personal spies, the focal position of the monarch as the centre of allegiance, and living symbol of the State, influenced language and imagery about the nature of government. But when in a period of years successive ministries of differing political hues might be in office, or even more radical changes in government—from constitutional monarchy, for example, to parliamentary republic to dictatorship—could occur without greatly altering day to day administration and policies, then people began to notice the specific organs of the State. These features have been particularly visible in France, and were noted by three nineteenth century thinkers of markedly different political tendencies: De Tocqueville, Marx and Kropotkin.

De Tocqueville comments at the end of his book on *The Old Régime and the French Revolution* that, after the first period of revolutionary enthusiasm and the spirit of freedom it generated, Napoleon's capture of power led to the salvaging of the institutions of the old régime and their integration into the new.

Centralization was built up anew, and in the process all that had once kept it within bounds was carefully eliminated . . . Napoleon fell but the more solid parts of his achievement lasted on; his government died, but his administration survived, and every time that an attempt is made to do away with absolutism the most that could be done has been to graft the head of Liberty onto a servile body (*The Old Régime*, 209).

Karl Marx writing on *The Eighteenth Brumaire of Napoleon Bonaparte* reached very similar conclusions :

This executive power, with its enormous bureaucratic and military organisation . . . which enmeshes the body of French society like a net and chokes all its pores, sprang up in the days of the absolute monarchy, with the decay of the feudal system, which it helped to hasten . . . Napoleon perfected this state machinery . . . All revolutions perfected this machine instead of smashing it (Marx and Engels, *Selected Works*, 170–1).

While Kropotkin illustrates his thesis on the State by reference to the Third French Republic, which 'in spite of its republican form of government, has remained monarchical in its essence'. How has this come about? Kropotkin answers :

It comes from France having remained as much a State as it was thirty years ago. The holders of power have changed their name; but all the immense scaffolding of centralised organisation, the imitation of the Rome of the Caesars which has been elaborated in France, has remained (*The State*, 42).

Bureaucracy

France has proved a useful model for generalizations about the modern State, and it also provides illustrations for a specific critique of bureaucracy. In their analysis of French bureaucracy De Tocqueville and Kropotkin converge. De Tocqueville draws on his knowledge of the *ançien régime* to develop his case—the damaging effects of the administration on the French economy, its inherent cumbersomeness and rigidity, its disregard of individual rights and of the law, and its enervating influence on social attitudes. In eighteenth century France Government inspectors made peasants tear up vines not planted in soil specified by official regulations; the Controller General in Paris had to decide the site of a workhouse hundreds of miles away, or regulate a village fête; a passion for building highways in perfectly straight lines led to the tearing down of houses

in the way and confiscation of land without just compensation; and
the Administration frequently overstepped its statutory powers; worst
of all local councillors became abjectly servile before central authority,
and every Frenchman became accustomed to the idea that the only
way to get things done was to petition Paris.

Looking at France at the turn of the century Kropotkin comments
that when a tree blows down on the National highway about fifty
documents have to be exchanged between the Home Office and the
Treasury before the tree can be sold. 'This is under the Third Republic, for I do not speak of the barbarous methods of the *ancien régime*
that limited itself to five or six documents.' But Kropotkin's concern,
like De Tocqueville's, goes much deeper :

> If it were only this, it would be but twenty thousand function-
> aries too many, and a thousand million francs more added to the
> budget . . . But there is worse beneath all this, for the *principle*
> kills everything. The peasants of a village have a thousand interests
> in common . . . But the State cannot allow them to unite ! It gives
> them school and priest, police and judge; these must suffice, and
> should other interests arise, they must apply in the regular way to
> Church and State (*The State*, 36).

Kropotkin adds that until 1883 villagers were forbidden by law to
unite even to irrigate their fields.

The notable increase in the size of central administration in all
'advanced' countries in this century has strengthened Kropotkin's
general case. Indeed some of the more obvious problems of bureaucracy have been acknowledged in both liberal and socialist democracies. Italy's overweighted civil service, for example, has long been
an incubus on the body politic, but since 1945 successive governments
have failed to achieve any civil service reforms. 'Nearly every
Government had appointed a special Minister whose job was "reform
of the Civil Service"; they had investigated and reported with more
or less diligence but with little effect. Every so often a scandal would
blow up to spur them on' (Muriel Grindiod, *Italy*, 155). Italy's civil
service is in part a product of inertia and corruption, and reflects
wider social and political problems. As Herbert Read once remarked :
'every country has the bureaucracy it deserves.' Max Weber, with
the example of Prussia before him, saw in the rationalization and
division of functions a method capable of managing large scale
economic and governmental enterprizes with considerable effectiveness.

But the potential efficiency of bureaucracy is undermined both by
a general tendency towards excess of red tape, and by the specific
problems of centralized economic planning. Modern industrial

Alexander Hertzin — Tolstoy

1. What is your relation, how do you view the philosophy of Che Guevara.

2. You mention Alex. Hertzin + Tolstoy do you see yourself as an anarchist in
the true sense of the word?

G. Menshen Hall 10th cent.

development appears both to require State intervention and to mul-
tiply the difficulties of central control—a fact which has led to the
French attempt at regionalism in economic planning. In the Soviet
Union 'the planners' task has become about one thousand times
more complex than it was when the first Five Year Plan was launched
in 1928. Indeed, one Soviet expert has estimated that if the planning
system were allowed to continue unchecked along its present lines,
by 1980 it would occupy every adult member of the population
(Erik De Mauny, *Russian Prospect*, 96). This trend has promoted
the limited measures of decentralization to regions and factories in
the mid-1950s, and the Liberman reforms introducing the profit
incentive in the 1960s. 'The Liberman reform has at least slowed
down the paper flood. Under the old system, forty to fifty of a
factory's "indicators" (directives on prices, delivery dates, production
schedules and so on) were handed down from above. Now, only five
or six are handed down' . . . (ibid.). Whether strictly controlled
decentralization and use of market mechanisms can do more than
mitigate bureaucratic chaos is still to be proven. But from an anarchist
standpoint both approaches are totally unsatisfactory in principle, and fail to trap resources of initiative and responsibility
which stem from free co-operation and participation in decision-
making.

The criteria for measuring a concept like 'efficiency' in relation to
bureaucratic and economic organization are far from unambiguous—
and in Kropotkin's approach they overlap with an assessment of the
total quality of social, cultural and personal life. It may be relevant
that where a serious movement away from bureaucratic centralism
has occurred in socialist countries, as in Yugoslavia, and briefly in
Czechoslovakia in 1968, narrowly defined questions of economic
efficiency have been closely related to issues of political and industrial
democracy, local autonomy and cultural freedom. The Anarchists'
main concern is certainly with the wider social implications of
bureaucracy. Herbert Read noted in 1938 in relation to the Soviet
Union that: 'since the revolution of 1917 the State machine has
year by year grown in size and importance . . . in the very process
of developing the power of the State new classes are born which
usurp this power and use it to oppress the people at large' (*Anarchy
and Order*, 94).

Alex Comfort remarks that centralized administration means a
proliferation of new laws and regulations, thus increasing the quantity of State defined 'crimes' in society. A sufficiently cumbersome
bureaucracy may not only impose rules people will want to break,
but rules which they are actually forced to break. This is the situation in Italy. In 1964 for example a former director of the Superior

g scientists, who
alleged that 'the antiquated condition of Italian administrative regulations makes scientific research impossible without some form of
evasion of the law', for example in procedures for ordering equipment
(*The Times*, 1 May 1964, 11). Soviet planning regulations have
similarly forced managers to improvise and co-operate in defiance of
the rules in order to fulfil their required quotas. The authorities have
turned a blind eye, but punished severely those who have taken
private enterprize too far. Erik De Mauny notes in relation to the
1963-4 Shakerman case that, after reading the trial records of the
complex transactions involved in building up an illegal commercial
empire, a Russian acquaintance commented: 'I wouldn't have put
him on trial—I'd have made him Minister of Finance!' (*Russian
Prospect*, 90).

Comfort is less concerned than Read about the power of a bureaucratic class, but is afraid that the effect of centralization of functions
and power is to provide opportunities for psychopathic leadership.
'The greater the degree of power, and the wider the gap between
governors and governed, the stronger the appeal of office to those who
are likely to abuse it, and the less the response which can be expected
from the individual' (*Authority and Delinquency in the Modern
State*, 75). In this connexion it is relevant to note that the new
German State created in the 1860s could boast an efficient civil
service, an efficient army and a booming economy: what it lacked
was a tradition of political responsibility and civil liberty—a lack
which manifested itself in the signal failure of the numerically strong
Social Democratic Party to challenge either State repression or German militarism. Max Weber saw in Bismark's Germany a type of
bureaucratic absolutism, in which the top officials tended to maintain a high degree of secrecy, and so become a power seeking clique
who were a law unto themselves.

Weber emphasized that the effects of bureaucracy in general on
the majority of its lesser officials was to encourage timidity, longing
for order, and narrowness of vision. When considering the implications of the trend to growing bureaucracy in all spheres of life he is
appalled:

> It is horrible to think that the world could one day be filled with
> nothing but those little cogs, little men clinging to little jobs and
> striving towards bigger ones ... It is as if in politics ... we were
> deliberately to become men who need 'order', and nothing but
> order ... and the great question is ... what can we oppose to this
> machinery in order to keep a portion of mankind free from this

parcelling-out of the soul, from this supreme mastery of the bureaucratic way of life (quoted in Reinhard Bendix, *Max Weber*, 464).

Weber, deeply committed to a code of aristocratic values (in which concepts of freedom and citizenship had a conservative and patriotic cast, but were linked to the constitutional tradition) was repelled partly by the pettiness of this mode of life, as De Tocqueville was repelled by the picture of 'democratic' uniformity in a centralized State.

The erosion of a sense of 'citizenship' among bureaucratic officials may have more directly sinister implications if conjoined to division of functions and the parcelling out of responsibility, since bureaucratic anonymity may allow men to commit atrocities they would never condone as individuals. Comfort comments that: 'The Policy-maker's assessment of the orders which he gives is blunted by the fact that he is separated from their physical execution—that of the executive by the fact that it is not responsible for them' (*Authority and Delinquency in the Modern State*, 61). Camus notes: 'One of the Dachau executioners weeps in prison and says, "I only obeyed orders. The Führer and Reichsführer, alone, planned all this . . . Gluecks received orders from Kaltenbrunner and, finally, I received orders . . ." ' (*The Rebel*, 151–2).

The worst perversions of bureaucracy occur however in conjunction with two other organs of State power deplored by anarchists: the military establishment and the police. In the economic and social spheres of government it is necessary to distinguish between anarchist criticisms and common liberal-conservative complaints about bureaucracy. The anarchist objection to 'welfare services' administered by civil servants, for example, is not that community welfare saps individual initiative and responsibility but that officially administered welfare is liable to be given inflexibly, officiously and heartlessly— objections envisaged by Kropotkin. Nor would anarchists subscribe to critiques of bureaucracy based primarily on judicial fears for the 'rule of law' or parliamentary fears about the lack of parliamentary control, though they might well agree that absence of adequate judicial and parliamentary checks increased the dangers of irresponsible use of power.

The spirit of De Tocqueville's attack on bureaucratic centralism is, however, closer to anarchist concerns, though his answer marks him sharply off from anarchism. De Tocqueville discovered in America and England a political alternative to State centralization, which led him to formulate a theoretical distinction between the spheres of 'government' and of 'administration'. There are, he suggests, certain interests common to a whole country, like passing general laws and securing defence : these interests may usefully be centralized. There are also local interests; to centralize these is to create a rigid and unwieldly centralized administration. Instead local affairs should be conducted through the political initiative of local citizens through municipal government and voluntary associations. Whether De Tocqueville's distinction between local and central interests, and between the role of voluntary associations and bureaucratic organizations, is still valid, and whether it can be maintained in practice, is best answered in relation to other features of State power, and in the light of historical developments since he wrote.

Police

A second feature of the State machinery of great importance for anarchists is a police force. While De Tocqueville is committed to the need for a government to maintain order, his comments on the role of mounted police under the *ançien régime* in France are pertinent :

> To the mind of the great majority of people only the government was capable of maintaining order in the land ... The mounted policeman was, in fact, the embodiment of law and order, not merely its chief defender ... No one seemed to have had the faintest inkling that the protector might one day become the master (*The Old Régime*, 69).

De Tocqueville then quotes the remarks of an uncomprehending French emigré in England on the absence of a military police : 'It is the literal truth that the average Englishman consoles himself for having been robbed with the reflection that his country has no mounted police !' It had obviously never occurred to him, comments De Tocqueville drily, that 'these "eccentricities" were bound up with the whole British concept of freedom.' But now an anarchist arguing against the existence of a police force is likely to be regarded with the same incredulity and condescension as the emigré then regarded the English.

It was in France under Napoleon that the organizational model of a modern political police was first created. Under Fouche, former Revolutionary Minister of Police, the Ministry of Police was reorganized in 1804 and provided an efficient instrument of surveillance and repression to maintain Napoleon in power. Fouché's department declined in influence after the fall of Napoleon, but many of its methods were retained by succeeding régimes, and the political police was strengthened again by Louis Napoleon to maintain his own dictatorship after 1851. After his fall the police under the Third Republic changed its leading personnel, but 'its functions altered little' (see E. K. Bramstedt, *Dictatorship and Political Police*, 48). Government ministers were reputed to live in fear of the dossiers of the police. In the early years of the Fourth Republic a public scandal revealed the bizarre workings of the rival secret services attached to the Ministry of the Interior and the Prime Minister's Office. Whilst the former was hushing up a scandal about the Socialist Party, the second in command of the latter was allegedly trying to frame two Socialist Ministers whom he wanted to have shot (see Philip Williams, *Politics in Post-War France*, 387). Nor is a secret police excluded by a tradition of liberalism. In 1965 an *Observer* article estimated there were police dossiers on two million political suspects in Britain.

Hannah Arendt comments that 'the secret services have rightly been called a state within the state, and this not only in despotisms but also under constitutional or semiconstitutional governments' (*The Origins of Totalitarianism*, 425). The dangers inherent in a specifically political police may also be seen as inherent in a normal police force. Ortega y Grasset urged in 1930 in *The Revolt of the Masses* that a concrete example of the dangers of the modern State crushing individual freedom was 'the enormous increase in the police force of all countries'. He goes on to predict that the police will not be content to maintain 'law and order' on the terms people want, but 'will end by themselves defining and deciding on the order they are going to impose' (94). It is a minor illustration of the link between aristocratic liberalism and anarchism that *Anarchy* uses a quote from this passage, together with Seymour Lipset's example of how police in the United States are publicly threatening to disobey orders which require police leniency towards black or student demonstrators (see Seymour Lipset, 'The Politics of the Police', *New Society*, 6 March 1969, and *Anarchy* No. 98, April 1969). De Jouvenel also comments with concern that: 'The growth of the police, in numbers, importance and dignity, is a universal phenomenon of the present time' (*Power*, 302).

The police role in maintaining public order necessarily tends to have political overtones. But suppression of 'crime' can in itself be seen as a form of political repression directed against the poor—especially when the highest crime rates occur in the poorest areas. It has been estimated, for example, that in communities in Western Sicily eight out of ten men have spent over a year in jail, and a further four per cent are outlaws (Gavin Maxwell, *The Ten Pains of Death*, 8). Slum dwellers or coloured minorities often feel that they are objects of automatic suspicion and fair game for any policeman.

Doubts about the category of crime are reinforced by the fact that both the investigations of the police, and the researches of social scientists, are usually directed—as a recent issue of *Anarchy* on criminology remarked—to 'lower working-class criminals' rather than to 'gangs' in the business and financial world (*Anarchy* No. 98).

Police are also placed in a position of unique opportunity and temptation to commit crimes themselves. One of the most frequent charges made against police is that of violent assault—widely publicized in certain cases of police violence against demonstrations, for example in Paris in May 1968 and in Chicago in August 1968 at the Democratic Party Convention. In recent years there has also been publicity in the United States about indiscriminate police shooting causing many deaths during 'riots' in black ghettos—which can be seen as a form of semi-political demonstration. But the most serious cases of police violence may be hidden from the public. Alex Comfort quotes from H. von Hentig, *The Criminal and His Victim*: 'The police force and the ranks of prison officers . . . afford legal channels for pain inflicting, power-wielding behaviour, and . . . confer upon their holders a large degree of immunity' (*Authority and Delinquency in the Modern State*, 38). A particularly extreme example is that of the police death squad in Brazil: in December 1969 a Rio de Janiero district police chief said he had evidence that members of the police were responsible for torturing and murdering 120 petty criminals in the previous two years (*The Times*, 10 December 1969, 7). Third degree methods are standard practice in many police forces —in France for example special expressions have been coined for the initial police interrogation. Britain has a better reputation. But the detective inspector who looked on while four men were beaten with a truncheon and rhino whip by two constables in Sheffield in March 1963 told an Inquiry 'these things go on fairly frequently, don't they', and apparently thought the victims were unlikely to complain, or to be believed if they did (Ben Whitaker, *The Police*, 148).

Where the level of violent crimes is exceptionally high, or gangsterism particularly well entrenched, the anarchist case for abolishing the police may be most persuasive. In the United States, for example, an official Commission on the Causes and Prevention of Violence has stressed that poverty is the main cause of the crime rate, and urged the need to completely rebuild American cities. Nor does the existence of a police force sufficiently reassure the large number of householders who fear to walk outdoors at night, or have invested in their own guns—a truly Hobbesian picture. Whilst in western sicily ruled by 'the Church, the State, and the Mafia' for decades, the most serious challenge to the Mafia has come from men working for radical social change. The Mafia shot forty-three trade unionists; and 'day labourers claiming the land, peasants taking part in Communist gatherings were met by rifle fire' (*The Times*, 26 February 1970, 11). But the direct action movement initiated by Danilo Dolci has survived intimidation and helped to uncover Mafia influence.

But in Sicily the Mafia is so closely linked to the powers-that-be that political resistance is appropriate; and poverty in the American ghettos is so closely linked to discrimination that social and economic measures are relevant. Where the social and political overtones of crime are less obvious, immediate political and social action becomes less plausible as an adequate response to the problem. Anarchists also confront the difficulty that, although a large proportion of crimes are committed by individuals or small groups, there are also highly organized and sometimes international crime syndicates. Crime, like big business, has tended to increase its organizational scale, and it poses for anarchists trusting in social change and community care of individuals something of the problem that Benjamin Tucker reluctantly came to acknowledge trusts, cartels and monopolies in the economic sphere created for his belief in totally free competition as an alternative to Government regulation (see the Postscript to sixth edition of *State Socialism and Anarchism*).

Whilst police forces are seen primarily as organs of the State, many aspects of police behaviour stem from the values of existing society. In Britain, for instance, *Anarchy* has pointed out that police now hunt down drug addicts with exceptional zeal. The difficulty of disentangling the operations of the State from the influence of the surrounding society is apparent in many anarchist writings. Their awareness of this relationship between the State and present society, and in particular the influence of a hierarchical class structure, leads anarchists to stress the need for fundamental social as well as political change. The importance of the social and economic context is particularly evident in discussions of the role of law and the operation of the legal system.

The Law

The anarchist view of law has been stated with great clarity and simplicity by Tolstoy. In his essay 'The Slavery of Our Times' he argues that the one characteristic common to all law is:

> that if any man does not fulfil them, those who have made these laws will send armed men, and the armed men will beat, deprive of freedom, or even kill, the man who does not obey the law— (*Essays from Tula*, 110).

Apart from being based on violence the law has two other characteristics which Tolstoy especially deplores—it is made in the interests
of the ruling class; and it involves mystification. In the course of
centuries millions of books have been written to explain what legislation is. According to this science of jurisprudence 'legislation is the
expression of the will of the whole people' (109). But 'everyone knows
that not in despotic countries only, but also in the countries nomin-
ally most free—England, America, France, and others—the laws are
made not by the will of all, but by the will of those who have
power, and therefore always and everywhere are such as are profit-
able to those who have power.' Tolstoy also detests the rituals and
procedures of courts. His hatred of the violence involved in law
enforcement and his contempt for the ritualism surrounding it fuse in
his passionate denunciation of capital punishment—for example in
his essay 'I Cannot Be Silent', which he wrote after reading in the
paper about the hanging of twelve men.

> Several peasants similar to those about to be hanged, but armed,
> dressed in clean soldiers' uniforms, with good boots on their feet,
> and with guns in their hands, accompany the condemned men.
> Beside them walks a long-haired man, wearing a stole and
> vestments of gold or silver cloth, and bearing a cross. The procession
> stops. The manager of the whole business says something; the
> secretary reads a paper; and when the paper has been read, the
> long-haired man, addressing those whom other people are about
> to strangle with cords, says something about God and Christ
> (*Essays from Tula*, 174).

Tolstoy then comes to the fourth element in his attack on law enforcement—the way in which direct responsibility is evaded by
subdividing the stages of passing the sentence and executing the
verdict, so that 'each may think and say it is not he who is responsible for them' (175).

Tolstoy's picture is a caricature, but like most caricatures it serves
to bring into prominence features often not noticed. There is a
frightening gap between the principles of legal theory and the actual
experience of the machinery of justice. This is true not only of the
Kafkaesque nature of a judicial organization, like that in Italy, which
may keep a man in jail for two years without trial; but of English
law, where the maxim that a person is to be held innocent until
proved guilty fits oddly with a system in which, if police refuse bail,
the accused may spend months in strict confinement, before a court
has convicted him.

James Baldwin has described in his essay 'Equal in Paris' his
farcical but terrifying experience of being arrested by mistake in

Paris for the theft of a hotel sheet (see *Notes of a Native Son*). The
legal machinery in which he was caught up involved the initial
interrogation 'quite chillingly clipped and efficient (so that there
was shortly no doubt in one's own mind that one should be treated
as a criminal', being fingerprinted and photographed, moved from a
cell to a communal shed in the Prefecture, and then driven in a police
wagon to a prison outside Paris, where he was locked in, 'divested
of shoelaces, belt, watch, money, papers, nailfile, in a freezing cell
in which both the window and toilet were broken with six other
adventurers'. Here he waited like the rest for the unknown day of
his trial, was told stories by his cell mates of men taken to be tried
being sent to the guillotine by mistake—'though I knew they were
teasing me it was simply not possible for me to totally disbelieve
them'—and after several days taken to court, where the lack of an
interpreter meant his case had to be postponed. Baldwin comments
on the proceedings :

> It seemed to me that all the sentences meted out that day were
> excessive; though, again, it seemed that all the people who were
> being sentenced that day had made, or clearly were going to make,
> crime their career. This seemed to be the opinion of the judge, who
> scarcely looked at the prisoners or listened to them; it seemed to be
> the opinion of the prisoners, who scarcely bothered to speak in
> their own behalf; it seemed to be the opinion of the lawyers, state
> lawyers for the most part, who were defending them. The great
> impulse of the courtroom seemed to be to put these people where
> they could not be seen ... (131).

Baldwin's account is not written in the directly polemical spirit
of Tolstoy's attacks on courts and jails, though it has in this passage
Tolstoyan overtones, which are even clearer in a later paragraph
where he describes how he went to Mass one Christmas day locked
in a cold cubicle and peering through an eye hole at 'an old Frenchman, hatted, overcoated, muffled and gloved, preaching in this language which I did not understand, to this row of wooden boxes, the
story of Jesus Christ's love for men'. But it is an unusually vivid
account of what happens daily to many less articulate men caught
up in due process of law. Some of Baldwin's helplessness arose from
his imperfect understanding of the language and ignorance of French
law. The average prisoner, however, confronted with legal jargon
and the complexities of legal and court procedures, is probably in
much the same position. Godwin commented bitterly on English
law :

> Law was originally devised, that ordinary men might know what
> they had to expect; and there is not, at this day, a lawyer existing

in Great Britain, vain-glorious enough to pretend that he has
mastered the code . . . It is a labyrinth without end; it is a mass
of contradictions that cannot be disentangled (*Enquiry Concerning
Political Justice*, Vol. II, 402).

Tolstoy underlines in his novel *Resurrection*, written after his
conversion to anarchism, how following the letter of the law and
the formalities of procedure may prevent genuine justice being done,
and the arbitrary element in judgments and in sentencing policy.
But the heart of his case is a conviction that the way the 'law' treats
people is humanly intolerable. James Baldwin recounts at the end of
his story of his prison experiences in Paris that when he finally came
before the court, having made contact with an attorney friend via
an ex-cell mate and been sent a lawyer, 'the story of the drap de lit,
finally told, caused great merriment in the courtroom.' He adds, 'I
was chilled by their merriment. It could only remind me of the
laughter I had often heard at home . . . This laughter is the laughter
of those who consider themselves to be at a safe remove from all the
wretched, for whom the pain of living is not real.' Durkheim's
aphorism about socialism—that it 'is not a science, a sociology in
miniature—it is a cry of grief, sometimes of anger . . .' (*Socialism*,
41). is perhaps more directly relevant to anarchism. But Durkheim's
concept of science leads him to overlook the fact that juxtaposing
experienced reality with theoretical abstractions and 'objective'
facts like legal codes is crucial to a serious sociology or theory of
politics. The anarchist is, in attacking the presuppositions of law,
speaking for large numbers of people, in particular the poor and in-
articulate, who, as Baldwin comments, have for the most part never
trusted legality.

There is an almost inescapable sense in which accepted theories of
politics and law are ideological justifications are for the existing
social hierarchy. They are largely accepted by those at the top who
make and administer the laws, and provide them with the principles
they need in the process; and these theories are often mutely or
openly rejected by those at the bottom, who see the 'law' from the
perspective of the police cell and the jail—to what extent those at
the bottom constitute a majority, and whether they comprise the
working class, does, however, vary considerably. The analysis of
jurisprudence as an ideology of the ruling class, put forward in simple
and popular terms by Marx and Engels in *The Communist Manifesto*,
is embraced by Tolstoy on the basis of his own observation. But this
view cannot be accepted as it stands for a number of reasons, one of
which was given by Engels in a letter written in 1890 trying to
explain the Marxist position on idealogy (Marx and Engels, *Selected*

Correspondence, 504–5). Engels argues that in the modern State law cannot simply be a reflection of economic relationships, or too blatantly an instrument of the ruling class, because as a legal system is elaborated it develops a life and logic of its own, and is constrained by the demands of internal consistency. A legal system has, therefore, an internal dynamic towards the realization of principles of equity and justice embodied within a legal code.

If we pursue the implications of Engels's qualifications about law as pure ideology we begin to arrive at a very strong case for seeking to maintain the role of law in society, at both a theoretical and immediately practical level. The existence of an elaborate set of procedures may be an important means of seeking redress for those abuses anarchists attack. Procedural rules help constrain all those involved in administering the law, and maintaining the rules may become a matter of professional pride. In addition, because any particular judicial system embodies general principles like protecting individual rights, it generates principles to which reformers can appeal in seeking to increase individual rights or to repeal unjust laws. The judiciary may also provide a certain bulwark of resistance against a government which seeks to exercise arbitrary and dictatorial powers. In South Africa for a long period the impartiality of judges in administering the law helped to mitigate the Government's drive against opponents of its apartheid policy. In Greece the extent of judicial resistance was indicated when the régime decided in May 1968 to depose twenty-one judges, a move Greece's Supreme Administrative Court declared illegal when the judges appealed.

As both South Africa and Greece show, strict application of the law can help maintain despotic laws and cruel penalties if the régime makes repressive laws, and can bypass safeguards in the existing law by allowing detention of prisoners for long periods without trial, or by setting up separate tribunals to try political prisoners. But the training and professional status of lawyers, magistrates and judges makes them less amenable to serving a dictatorship than either the administrative bureaucracy or police, and to regard the judiciary in all circumstances simply as an organ of the State is a rather dangerous simplification. Members of the judiciary also inherit a set of values on which to base a wider political resistance. The professor of Penal Law at Athens University, dismissed in a political purge in 1969 and later arrested, said in a farewell lecture on the spirit and essence of law :

The fundamental value towards which it is oriented is freedom . . .
If the lawyer forgets this, he becomes a mere technician, an
instrument of oppression in the hands of the strong . . . My

separation from you now is the price I must pay for adhering to
the values I have venerated all my life (*The Guardian*, 24 February
1969, 3).

That the model of legality and justice enshrined in laws and courts
has genuine meaning is demonstrated by our ability to recognize
'mockeries of justice', which flout not only the principles but the
procedures of fair trail. Herbert Read comments that Justice, in her
ancient personification, is blind and holdng a pair of scales. Though
the idea of retribution, represented by the sword of Justice, has come
to dominate, the original conception is retained in 'the very precious
independence of the judiciary. That independence may by now be
more in name than in substance, but at any rate it is a recognition
of distinct values' (*Anarchy and Order*, 188). Read then reverts to a
more familiar anarchist position, noting that the independence of the
judiciary is symbolized by its wigs and gowns and rituals which
create 'a shell of custom and formality', which excludes all direct
human response and human values.

Anarchists can quite consistently recognize the possible value of
judicial independence within existing States, but maintain that in a
new and better society the defensive role of the judiciary against the
State would be unnecessary. In the revolutionary tradition stemming
from the French Revolution abolition of the old courts is usually
seen as a necessary stage in achieving a new society. But denial of
judicial independence has proved to have its dangers in practice. De
Jouvenel quotes Faguet, *Le Libéralisme* :

> 'The subordination of the magistracy to the government is one of
> the triumphs of the Revolution. At the moment of proclaiming
> the rights of man, it destroyed their castle and paralysed their
> defenders.' (*Power*, 197).

More recent experience in socialist countries has shown that once
application of the law is legitimately subject to political direction, it
is also directly vulnerable to the pressures which arise in the political
process itself. From an anarchist standpoint, however, the history of
the countries where Communist Parties have come to power reinforces
their belief in the necessity of abolishing the State and avoiding the
creation of a new government authority.

Authority and Government

The anarchist attitude to law is very closely related to the wider
question of the role of government in society, and the meaning of
legitimate authority. It is on these issues that anarchists tend to part

company altogether with the constitutional theorists. Law combines authority—embodied in certain persons, denoted by rituals, and often hallowed by age—with a strictly defined use of force designed to protect society. Legitimate governments likewise derive the authority vested in them from adherence to certain procedures in obtaining power, and from using their power only in modes defined by custom or the constitution. As in the case of law courts, the authority of governments is usually enhanced by ritual ceremonies and insignia of office—this was especially true of monarchs who came to the throne through the pageantry of a coronation and spent their lives amid the etiquette of courts. In Europe kings were crowned by bishops, and the ritual of their office was often interwoven with church rituals. It is partly because the spiritual authority of the Church has so often reinforced the temporal authority of the ruler that anarchists tend to be so antagonistic to the Church as the handmaid of earthly powers.

But opposition to religion is closely related to a general opposition to regalia, symbols, ceremonies and beliefs which encourage people to venerate government. Tolstoy, for instance, is always anxious to strip the Emperor of his clothes and reveal the naked violence underneath. He seizes on an article written for a Budapest paper, *Ohne Staat*, which led to the prosecution of its author, Eugen Schmitt, for saying that 'Governments, justifying their existence on the ground that they ensure a certain kind of safety to their subjects, are like the Calabrian robber-chief who collected a regular tax from all who wished to travel in safety along the highways' (*Essays from Tula*, 124–5). This is perfectly true, Tolstoy comments, except that the robber-chief is morally superior to governments who plunder not the rich but the poor, who, unlike the brigand, never take personal risks, and who do not rely on voluntary recruits to their band, but often enrol their soldiers by force.

Tolstoy's objections to symbols and ceremonies in both government and the Church is also a rationalist objection to the paraphernalia and superstitions cluttering up mens' minds, and obscuring the clear and simple solutions of reason and common sense. Godwin attacks the mystique of office for similar reasons. But Godwin himself partly suggests in *Political Justice* the potential value of such symbols of authority :

In the riots in the year 1780, the mace of the house of lords was proposed to be sent into the passages, by the terror of its appearance to quiet the confusion; but it was observed that, if the mace should be rudely detained by the rioters, the whole would be thrown into anarchy (Vol. II, 54–5).

This passage is reminiscent of Madame De Stael's comments on the Constituent Assembly, which believed 'there was some magic in its decrees'.

> But its pronouncements can be compared to the ribbon which had been drawn through the garden of the Tuileries to keep the people at some distance from the palace . . . (gusted in Bertrand de Jouvenel, *The Pure Theory of Politics*, 36).

When people ceased to respect this barrier it became meaningless. When Napoleon broke up the Assembly with soldiers and publicly humiliated its members, he exposed the fragility of conventions protecting parliamentary immunity. De Jouvenel comments wryly, 'Indeed the law is a mere ribbon' (37).

Symbols and ceremonials have always surrounded government, as De Jouvenel stresses, not only in nation states but in tribal communities, ancient city republics and feudal kingdoms. They impress upon those holding power the gravity and responsibilities of their office; they encourage people to respect authority; and they discourage usurpers from seeking to seize power. The existence of respected procedures for the transfer of power is exceptionally hard to achieve. Under kings the problem was at last partially resolved by making the throne hereditary. Electoral and parliamentary rituals now fulfil the role in liberal democracies of denoting the legitimacy of government, and ensuring a peaceful transition of power. Where no such procedures exist, or are not generally respected, power becomes the prize of the most ruthless conspirator, the man controlling the army or police or party apparatus, or whoever is prepared to foment civil war.

Proudhon in an interesting passage in *The Federative Principle* recognizes the general value of oaths and ceremonies performed in public in binding individuals to perform the duties of the role, or office, they are about to undertake. Proudhon, unlike most anarchists, sees a positive value in a marriage ceremony. He supports for the same reasons the taking of oaths by witnesses and arbitrators, and, by extension of his reasoning, public oaths by public officials. Proudhon makes, however, a sharp distinction between a contract among individuals, or an undertaking to society as a whole, and an oath of fealty or submission to higher authority. Whilst anarchists might admit the value of custom and ritual to promote a sense of responsibility, they naturally reject the value of ceremony designed to promote respect and obedience to government. Alex Comfort comments in *Authority and Delinquency in the Modern State* that 'Obedience in modern societies is more often a hideous vice than a Christian virtue' (83); elsewhere he states that 'Every atrocity of the war was the direct consequence of somebody obeying when he should have thought' (*Art and Social Responsibility*, 83). Ceremonials of legitimacy may also blind people to quite illegitimate usurpations or abuses of power, as Proudhon continuously tried to show in his critique of universal suffrage. The anarchist suspicion of the mystique surrounding power is reinforced by the sense that it may be a secularized outlet for religious emotion. Herbert Read drew attention to the fact that after twenty years of socialism in Russia, 'the deification of Lenin (sacred tomb, effigies, creation of a legend—all the elements are there) is a deliberate attempt to create an outlet for religious emotions' (*Anarchy and Order*, 45). Stalin, whilst he was alive, had statues of himself erected throughout his domain in a manner reminiscent of the Roman Emperors—a feature of what has been aptly termed the personality cult.

Revolutionaries have always felt the need of their own symbolism. In 1959 in Hungary the giant-sized statue of Stalin was smashed from its pedestal. In 1871 the Paris Commune to 'mark the new era of history it was conscious of initiating . . . pulled down that collosal symbol of martial glory, the Vendome column' (Marx, *The Civil War in France, Selected Works*, 297). Anarchists themselves often symbolize their allegiance by black and red flags. Symbolism, ceremonial and imagery appear to be intrinsic to political activity, though they may not always be flamboyant. In the republican and constitutionalist strand of European thought there have always been two dominating and contrasting images : on the one hand an 'oriental' despotism, in which a man claiming godlike powers towers over his abject subjects and rules according to personal caprice through arbitrary violence; on the other a polity of equals, in which free citizens fear no one but respect the laws, and share with their peers the risks, responsibilities and privileges of governing. These images are both captured in a speech Shakespeare puts into the mouth of Cassius at a time when republicanism is crumbling before Caesarism. Cassius is urging Brutus to resist Caesar's ambitions :

> Why, man, he doth bestride the narrow world
> Like a Colossus; and we petty men
> Walk under his huge legs, and peep about
> To find ourselves dishonourable graves . . .
> When could they say, till now, that talk'd of Rome
> That her wide walls encompas'd but one man?
>
> (*Julius Caesar*, Act I, Scene II.)

This image of republican liberty has both its aristocratic and democratic interpretations. De Jouvenel, who stresses the former, comments that 'Brutus' dagger, so dear to the Jacobin heart, was

wielded by an aristocratic hand' (*Power*, 277). The Constitutionalist
thinkers have tended to superimpose the aristocratic version of republicanism upon feudal Europe, in which freedom was guaranteed by
customary laws, independent local communes and guilds, and a
proud aristocracy of peers prepared to fight for their privileges, or
liberties, against the incursions of royal power. Theorists who accept
this picture tend to stress the significance of rule of law, balance of
powers and of federalism as means of curbing despotic government.
De Tocqueville inherits this constitutionalism, but has both the
sensitivity to democratic values and the social realism to seek to
transform these models into a picture compatible with modern
society. In America he finds a possible answer—a federal constitution, further decentralized by the existence of vigorous local governments able to administer their own affairs, and rooted in the custom
of the town meeting; a general habit of creating voluntary associations for social purposes; a free and localized press; and a widespread
respect for the laws and the constitution.

In the picture of a liberal society espoused by De Tocqueville and
later constitutional theorists parliamentary institutions have a role
quite distinct from that of democratic respresentation. In its historical
evolution in England, parliament acted as a check on arbitrary
power, and a public forum for grievances, while extending to its
members a privilege and immunity which enabled them to attack the
administration. The change from government by the king to government by the leaders of the major party has not substantially altered
the role of parliament as a whole, though the fact that voters may
throw out the ruling party can, with qualifications, be seen as an
additional check on misuse of power. In America the constitution
enshrined this function of the legislature as a check on the elected
president through division of powers. In a society equipped with the
traditions and institutional safeguards of personal liberty, a representative assembly may be seen as an added bulwark of liberty against
the State.

If democratic concepts are grafted onto a parliamentary institution one theory of representation which emerges is that of the representation of interests—the prevailing notion in eighteenth century
England. Representatioin of individual or group interests by a parliamentary advocate prepared to plead a case is quite compatible with
the constitutional nature of parliament in principle (though in
practice powerful pressure groups may harness government power to
their own ends). This concept of representation is not necessarily
'democratic' and is quite distinct from the idea that an elected
assembly represents the 'will of the people', which, whether this
'will' is viewed individually or collectively, is impossible—except in

Hobbes's purely formal sense. It is this myth-making conception of representation, and the related idea of sovereignty, that Proudhon attacked, arguing that government by the grace of the people was replacing government by the grace of God, and the idol of the people being enthroned in place of the idol of the king. Moreover, said Proudhon, the supposed delegate of the sovereign people will always become the master. Whether parliamentary assemblies usurp, through the ritual of elections, the interpretation of the general will, or a dictator usurps it from parliament through the magic of a plebiscite, the concept of 'sovereign will' provides a justification for centralized power and for sweeping aside all barriers to the exercise of this power. So 'democracy' may threaten liberty. It was an alternative to the French theory of democratic sovereignty that De Tocqueville sought, and believed he had found, in America. Proudhon likewise bitterly compared the French people, hemmed in like a prisoner in a cell, with the Americans who 'have no police, no centralisation, no army; who have not any government in the same sense attached to this term in antiquity' (*La Revolution Sociale*, 24).

De Tocqueville would not, however, have entirely accepted this picture. In the context of federalism, decentralism and constitutional liberty he admires a strong government, which he believed the Americans possessed.

> As all persons must have recourse to certain grammatical forms which are the foundations of human language, in order to express their thoughts; so all communities are obliged to secure their existence by submitting to a certain amount of authority, without which they fall into anarchy (*Democracy in America*, Vol. 1, 70).

Elsewhere De Tocqueville underlines that power in itself is not necessarily harmful : 'Men are not corrupted by the exercise of power, or debased by the habit of obedience; but by the exercise of a power which they believe to be illegitimate, and by obedience to a rule which they consider to be usurped and oppressive' (Vol. I, 9).

It is interesting to contrast Kropotkin on the society envisaged by anarchism : 'It seeks the most complete development of individuality combined with the highest development of voluntary association in all its aspects . . . A society to which preestablished forms, crystallized by law, are repugnant.' Later in the same pamphlet, *Anarchism: Its Philosophy and Ideal*, he comments :

> Far from living in a world of visions and imagining men better than they are, we see them as they are; and that is why we affirm that the best of men is made essentially bad by the exercise of authority and that the theory of the 'balancing of powers' and

'control of authorities' is a hypocritical formula, invented by those
who have seized power, to make the 'sovereign people', whom they
despise, believe that the people themselves are governing (7–8).

In this passage Kropotkin attacks both the constitutionalist and
democratic theories of government, which have tended to merge in
practice; his rejection of the approach to government espoused by
De Tocqueville is complete.

Both De Tocqueville and Kropotkin developed their political ideas
out of historical scholarship (which united them in admiration for
the medieval cities) and an awareness of social diversity. The most
appropriate way to assess their respective positions is to consider
historical developments since they wrote. Twentieth-century experience to date suggests that while Kropotkin's optimism for the evolution of anarchist society was unfounded, De Tocqueville's hope for
limited government in a free and constitutional society has not been
fulfilled either, least of all in America. His distinctions between
voluntary association and bureaucratic control, and between local and
central administration, have become blurred due to institutional,
economic, technological and political developments.

Modern Society

Bureaucratic modes of organization are, as Weber predicted, affect-
ing many non-governmental spheres—industry, universities, scientific research, and communications media. Horowitz includes in his
collection of writings *The Anarchists*, an essay by Robert Presthus
on the deadening effect of giant organizations on research and
creativity, and the ironing out of individuality in favour of an
organization man. 'Bureaucratization plays its part relentlessly as the
trend towards spending one's work life in a single organization . . .
In sum, big organizations typically seek control, discipline, and
standardization' (555). In a much more radical analysis ('Presthus is
so far from being an anarchist that he is mainly concerned the
United States may be falling behind the Soviet Union in the arms
race') John McDermott argued in *The Nation* (14 April, 1969) that
rapid technical progress has meant the development of giant instiu-
tions applying this knowledge. This development has been pioneered
in the sphere of defence, but applies to all aspects of American life :
economic corporations, universities and foundations as well as government agencies. The result, McDermott suggests, has been to render
almost meaningless the old distinctions between public and private,
industrial and educational, military and civilian. He gives as examples :

A company like RCA manages missile tracking systems, does research in linear algebra, edits and markets new novels, plans new educational systems, and experiments with electronic music. The University of Michigan, another growing corporate, teaches students at Ann Arbor, advises welfare mothers in Detroit, and pacifies peasants in Thailand ... America believes in *progress*. Hence it gives free rein to those very large organizations which have mastered *technology*, calling this *pluralism* (458–9).

There has also been a major expansion of centralized administration for largely economic reasons : the depression of the inter-war years, the subsequent influence of Keynesian economic theory, and the scale of modern technology have promoted State intervention in the economy even by governments ideologically averse to 'planning'. Development of welfare programmes has also tended to strengthen central administration, even if detailed application has been delegated to local agencies. Government involvement is linked to a centralizing tendency within the business world itself. Paul Goodman comments, in *People or Personnel* on the situation in the United States :

> The warring trusts have settled into a system of semi-monopolies, with fixed prices, for mutual security. The free market has turned into a synthetic creature of advertising. Government has entered into colossal alliances : in real estate, with municipalities and promoters; in agriculture, with giant croppers and grocery chains; in science and education, with the universities and high-technology corporations; in highways, with automobile manufacturers and oil men (45).

Automation and cybernetics suggest that in the future there will be even greater pressures towards central planning in order to avoid mass unemployment. This possibility of State planning for mass welfare and leisure in a society dominated by technology threatens both individual freedom and models of social action at a level so far mostly explored in the realms of science fiction rather than political theory. The somewhat incoherent concept of 'mass society' attempts to chart the early stages of this process, for example in relation to the mass media.

Fourthly, there is widespread concern that representative assemblies are unable to exert any real check on the actions of government or the organs of the State, and that the electorate is apathetic about elections and parliamentary politics. One school of thought associated with Schumpeter has reinterpreted democratic theory to square with present reality, in effect accepting Proudhon's view that 'democracy' only means choosing every few years between sets of rulers. This concept of democracy based on competing *élites* encourages the theory—advanced, for example, by Lazarsfeld and his colleagues on the basis of their voting studies in the United States—that apathy is a sign of political well-being, since it denotes satisfaction and promotes stability.

But in the republican tradition of political thought political activity has always been associated with freedom, and inactivity with despotism—albeit perhaps a mild and even enlightened despotism. De Tocqueville suggests in relation to the cities of the *ancien régime*, that sham rituals were rejected when their reality had been lost:

> Not so easily hoodwinked as many have imagined, the 'common people' ceased to take any active part in local government . . . In towns where a semblance of free elections had been retained [the ordinary citizen] was pressed to the voting urns, but he usually preferred to stay at home. Every student of history knows that this phenomenon is a common one; rulers who destroy men's freedom commonly begin by trying to retain its forms . . . (*The Old Régime*, 45).

Herbert Read comments on the apathy of voters in parliamentary democracies that it is due to 'this very process of centralization and collectivization which is taking place independently' (*Anarchy and Order*, 104).

War and the State

The tendencies towards giant-sized organization, State co-ordination with big business. dominance of technology and the erosion of traditional political safeguards are epitomized and promoted by a fifth factor—war and national defence. The two World Wars have had a lasting impact on the State. Even more significant is the entrenchment of major military establishments in a time of nominal peace—a development particularly noticeable in the United States, remarkably free from military pressures prior to the First World War and even the Second. De Tocqueville himself noted that America was in the nineteenth century favoured by being secure from military attack, and so free from military burdens and the threat of military ambitions. He also saw the importance of war in hastening centralization:

> No protracted war can fail to endanger the freedom of a demo-
> cratic country . . . War does not always give over countries to
> military government, but it must invariably and immeasurably

increase the powers of civil government; it must almost
compulsorily concentrate the direction of all men and the
management of all things in the hands of the administration
(*Democracy in America*, Vol. II, 268–9).

Randolph Bourne, best known among anarchists for his unfinished
essay on the State, coined the phrase 'war is the health of the State'.

The nation in war-time attains a uniformity of feeling, a hierarchy
of values culminating at the undisputed apex of the State ideal,
which could not possibly be produced through any other agency
than war (quoted in H. W. Morton, 'Randolph Bourne vs. the
State', *Anarchy*, No. 31, September 1963, 265).

If the effects of cold war are less startling, they are also more pro-
longed. Massive investment in armaments, a major bureaucracy
administering the instruments of destruction and the extensive
activities of the Central Intelligence Agency, which takes in 'business firms and institutions seemingly private' and 'many domestic
activities, from broadcasting stations and a steamship company to the
university campus' (David Wise and Thomas B. Ross *The Invisible
Government*, 4–5), have dominated American politics for twenty
years and show no sign of diminishing. The role of law as a check
on State power or safeguard of individual freedom and constitutional
liberties is also least effective in relation to military policies which
demand the predominance of 'security'. In Britain campaigners for
nuclear disarmament and in the United States protesters against the
Vietnam War have tried unsuccessfully to challenge in the courts
the assumption that government policy is necessarily against the
interest and security of the State. Moreover, military requirements
may promote legislation with very iliberal implications, like the
Emergency Laws recently passed in West Germany. Allen Dulles
commented that the American 1947 National Security Act had 'given
Intelligence a more influential position in our government than
Intelligence enjoys in any other government of the world' (*The
Invisible Government*, 4).
  The war-making powers of the State have always greatly pre-
occupied anarchists. Godwin observed that war has 'been found the
inseparable ally of political institutions'. But in this century war
has become a dominant theme in anarchist writing. Read comments:

War increases in intensity and effect as society develops its central
organization . . . this problem of war and peace . . . has been an
obsession with my generation. There is no problem which leads
so inevitably to anarchism (*Anarchy and Order*, 120–1).

Geoffrey Ostergaard writing in *Anarchy* claims that 'the omni-present threat of nuclear annihilation now clearly vindicates the anti-statism of the anarchists and the syndicates. For war is a func-tion of the state and the state system into which mankind is politic-ally divided' (No. 28, June 1963, 184).

De Jouvenel too relates State centralization to modern war. Writing *Power* under the impression of the horrors of the Second World War he quotes Montesquieu's warning on the danger of large armies: 'And soon having soldiers will result in having nothing but soldiers, and we shall become like the Tartars' '18). He goes on to document the development of total war from the time of the French Revolution, which ushered in conscription to the total moblization of whole populations in the Second World War. Alex Comfort, also writing immediately after the last War, comments in *Art and Social Responsibility* that 'barbarian society is rooted today in obedience, conformity, conscription . . .' (83).

Constitutionalist Theory and Anarchism

The link between constitutionalist theory and anarchist theory exists not only at an analytical level but in their common adherence to certain values: the value of local community realized through a wide range of independent associations; the value of individual free-dom usually seen in terms of social activity and as inseparable from a sense of responsibility to society; and, sometimes, a sense of belong-ing to a minority, or 'aristocracy', and a related sense of pessimism about achieving more than integrity in action. Paul Goodman notes the anarchist elements in the thought of Madison, writing on the experimental values of decentralism; and quotes Jefferson: 'A little rebellion now and then is a good thing . . . This truth should render republican governors so mild in their punishment of rebellions as not to discourage them' (*People or Personnel*, 33). Goodman also sug-gests that after the American Revolution society remained organized in fairly autonomous communities and associations which, in rela-tion to State or Federal Government 'existed in a virtual community-anarchy' (32). They were not, however, non-political; the independent élite especially 'regarded themselves as a band of citizen-friends born to make institutions, constitutions or whatever' (33). It is this image of pluralism, reproduced with qualifications by De Tocqueville in 1830 in *Democracy in America*, which has continuing appeal for many in the anarchist tradition. Colin Ward quoting G. D. H. Cole expresses sympathy with pluralistic ideas and suggests their rele-vance to modern Western Society (*Anarchy*, No. 14, April 1962).

The connexions between this conception of pluralism and the 'pluralism' of big corporations and pressure group politics, often endorsed in American political science, is purely rhetorical.

Richard Drinnon in his biography of Emma Goldman, in the course of which he notes the switch in America from 'vigilante authoritarianism', hostile to all radical agitation, to 'bureaucratic authoritarianism'; demonstrated by the growing power of the Bureau of Investigation after the First World War, stresses the anarchist emphasis on individual freedom. Drinnon comments:

> From the standpoint of the general Western liberal tradition, the anarchism for which Emma stood is perhaps superior ethically to any other political theory. No other theory makes so primary an appeal to the individual responsibility and intelligent self-expression of man ... Emma Goldman had the early and relatively rare insight that responsible individual freedom is the touchstone of supreme importance in the modern world (*Rebel in Paradise*, 111).

The primacy of the value of 'freedom' is also suggested by George Molnar in a review of Woodcock's survey of anarchism. Molnar concludes:

> Anarchism has certain features in common with socialism, populism, etc. It is distinguished from them by being the only radical movement whose principal avowed concern was with freedom ... Freedom is not something to which the world can be converted; it is of its nature a minority interest (*Anarchy*, No. 28, June 1963, 169).

The crucial distinction between all forms of liberalism and all forms of anarchism is reflected in the phrase 'radical movement'. Liberals who feel attached to the constitutionalist tradition tend in practice to support existing parliamentary and party politics, partly on the grounds that the likely alternatives are very much worse. They rely on the 'rule of law' as one of the main bulwarks of freedom, and so deplore all forms of unconstitutional and illegal action. Their adherence to pluralism leads them to oppose State intervention in the economic sphere designed to *replace* or closely control existing business corporations, so the opposition to socialism entailed in De Tocqueville's views is now even more pronounced. And a distrust of all proposals for sweeping social change or 'fanatical' utopianism leads many modern constitutionalists to adopt in relation to modern society an inherently conservative stance. Some of the values and ideas held by anarchists may link up with 'conservative' ideology—Goodman comments that the 'gentlemen of the Right, who invented the protective tariff and the trusts, now complain in Populist terms that liberty is encroached on' (*People and Personnel*, 48). But the interpretation is totally different.

Anarchists who may accept some of De Tocqueville's key values reinterpret them in a radical style of politics. Local community is seen not simply as a desirable intermediary between the individual and the State, but as the basis for a society totally free of any State organization. The local community is also seen as a base for direct action for social change—housing the homeless, experimenting in workers' control, creating local associations to build a better environment. Anarchist freedom is linked to a concept of citizenship which demands direct resistance to the State, and civil disobedience as the fulfilment of responsible citizenship. And anarchists, despite their disillusionment with the State socialism inaugurated by Marxist parties in power, usually ally themselves with the ideals and goals of the socialist movement.

In view of the trends which have in this century tended to destroy genuine social pluralism based on local independence and voluntary initiative, to reduce the role of law in protecting individual freedom, and to extend the power of the police and military organs of the State, De Tocqueville's ideal of liberty and community does appear to demand in Western society resistance to the war-making powers of the State in particular, and a restructuring of the institutions of modern society. The case for a 'radical' reinterpretation of constitutionalist values appears particularly strong in the country De Tocqueville hoped would escape the ills of centralization—the United States. Though if we are looking at America in concrete terms, and not simply treating it as a model of the trends in Western society, it is important to recognize the degree to which the Senate or the Supreme Court may still act to oppose the administration, and the significant areas of liberty which exist (for example freedom for political propaganda in the armed forces) alongside striking illiberalism. Secondly, the sheer size and great power status of the United States are clearly relevant. An extreme anarchist case for 'revolution' is less persuasive in smaller countries like the Scandinavian liberal democracies; though the greater degree of democracy, liberty and equality their citizens enjoy constitute a strong argument in favour of the general anarchist plea for decentralism.

The nation State is now apparently undergoing further transformation, especially in Western Europe where it has existed longest. Economic and technical factors are breaking down national frontiers in favour of larger economic units, and technical developments in warfare have greatly reduced the military significance of national boundaries. These considerations do not, however, invalidate the anarchist critique of the State; on the contrary they suggest that both anarchist proposals for confederation based on the power of local communities, and the anarchist scepticism about the merits or inevitability of industrial and technical 'progress', have great contemporary relevance. If it can be argued persuasively that the anarchist critique of the State and modern society is becoming more, rather than less, relevant, it remains to consider the nature of the alternative anarchist society.

3   Anarchism and Society

The Paris Commune

The anarchist alternative to State control based on repression is a
self-regulating social order. What an anarchist society would be like
has been indicated primarily by Proudhon, Bakunin and Kropotkin,
who despite significant differences share certain common values, and
who all three define their position to some extent in opposition
to Marxist socialism. Any comparison with Marxism is rendered
difficult by the inherent diversity of the anarchist tradition, including
the very divergent interpretations of Proudhon and Bakunin available and the increasing complexity of Marxism as it has evolved.
But since anarchism has been engaged in a conscious critique of
Marxism for over a century comparison is clearly relevant. Both
start off with a common commitment to abolish capitalism and the
capitalist State; both reject parliamentary liberalism; and both aspire
to create a society free from inequality and exploitation. Where they
often differ is in their attitudes to nationalism, industrialization and
democracy, and so in their conceptions of historical progress. The
crucial point of difference is on the role of State power in the tran-
sitional period after a socialist revolution. Ultimately they also dis-
agree on the role of government and of law, and in their understanding of 'politics'.

Many of the differences between Marxists and anarchists emerge
interestingly in their views of the 1871 Paris Commune, adopted
by both as a symbol of the new socialist society—focussing on the
Commune means comparing the most libertarian element in Marxist
thinking about post-revolutionary organization with anarchism.
For Marxists the Commune symbolizes a type of participatory
democracy which draws on the French Revolutionary idea of popular
sovereignty, but seeks to realize it through a combination of radical
decentralism and populist devices. The Commune which rose phoenix-
like out of the destruction of Louis Napoleon's Empire was in Marx's
eyes the antithesis of the previous imperial power—'the centralized
state power with its ubiquitous organs of standing army, police,
bureaucracy, clergy and judicature'. The model of communal government in Paris was intended to be a pattern for the rest of the
country, 'even the smallest hamlet', to follow. The Commune guarded

itself against the domination of the organs of the new 'state' over society by what Engels called 'two infallible means':

> In the first place, it filled all posts—administrative, judicial and educational—by election on the basis of universal suffrage of all concerned, subject to the right of recall at any time by the same electors. And, in the second place, all officials, high or low, were paid only the wages received by other workers (Marx and Engels, *Selected Works*, 261–2).

The Marxist commitment to radical popular sovereignty also entails contempt for constitutionalist devices like balance of powers, separation of functions and the hedging of central power through local autonomy or federalism. Marx commended the Commune for abolishing the distinction between legislature and executive, between policy-making and administration: 'The Commune was to be a working, not a parliamentary, body, executive and legislative at the same time' (291). He attacked the view that the Commune was a reversion to the medieval commune, commenting that the local communes which were an inheritance from feudalism had been in France converted effectively into a 'substratum' of modern State power, and that in Prussia the municipal constitution had degraded the town governments to 'mere secondary wheels in the police-machinery of the Prussian State' (293). He also denied that the Commune represented 'an attempt to break up into a federation of small states, as dreamed of by Montesquieu and the Girondins', or 'an exaggerated form of the ancient struggle against overcentralisation' (293). Constitutionalist theorists' admiration for England, where the logic of state centralization has been impeded, is derided; corrupt local government in the towns and 'virtually hereditary magistrates in the counties' simply 'complete the great central State organs'.

Federalism and Nationalism

Marx was necessarily committed to abolishing institutions which embodied the practices of a previous régime, and rightly emphasised the distinctively new character of the Commune. But his opposition to 'federalism' raises questions about the *direction* of revolutionary change. It is on this point anarchists have always taken issue with Marxists, and it is relevant that Marx's pamphlet on *The Civil War in France* is in a sense 'claiming' the Commune for the First International, and implicitly discrediting the Proudhonist claims to it as an embodiment of their own theories of confederation. Marx stresses that 'the unity of the nation was not to be broken', and 'the few

but important functions which still would remain for a central
government were not to be suppressed, as has been intentionally mis-
stated . . .' (292). Lenin takes up this question in *The State and
Revolution* :

> To confuse Marx's views on the 'destruction of the state power—
> the parasitic excrescence' with Proudhon's federalism is positively
> monstrous ! . . . Federalism as a principle follows logically from
> the petty-bourgeois views of anarchism. Marx was a centralist
> (89–91).

Proudhon too was scornful about constitutionalist devices like the
balance of power and the separation of the legislature and the executive, when these are a disguise for an underlying drive to maximize
the power of the State itself, as in the 1848 Constitution in France.
He also deplores the use made by Rousseau of the distinction between
framing and executing the laws, since Rousseau is led to posit the
need for a permanent executive which by its very nature will tend
to usurp power from the people legislating as a body. However,
Proudhon also hails the principle of the balance and separation of
powers as a great invention if its potential implications can be
extended to demolish unified and centralized State power. He suggests that the balance of power at the centre of the State should be
replaced by a federative contract in which each commune, canton,
province and region retains more power than it surrenders to the
higher level; and that the division of power should be extended to
functional separation of powers between different branches of industry.

Proudhon's federalism stems not only from a general belief in
local autonomy but also from acute distrust of new nationalisms.
He argues that many nationalist movements aspiring to create new
nation States are based on the historical claims of old kingdoms or
empires, and so embody a desire towards nationalist domination. His
book on *The Federative Principle* is particularly critical of Italian
nationalism for its lack of concern for the economic emancipation of
the peasants, and its willingness to subordinate republican principles to the *real politik* demands of national unification under the
Piedmontese King. Proudhon tries to distinguish between imperalistic
forms of nationalism, and a concept of nationality based on culture,
tradition and geographical factors, which would favour regionalism
in Italy rather than a unified State. Proudhon's own brand of ardent
patriotism is rooted first in his regional loyalty to the France-Comté.
His belief in regional 'nationalism' is also entirely consistent with
his advocacy of confederation. Nevertheless, his patriotism, allied to
his insensitivity to the nationalist aspiration of others, led some of

his contemporaries to accuse him of, in effect, promoting the national interests of France. While Marx commented that Proudhon's attack on Polish nationalism in its struggle against Russia led to his writing 'for the greater glory of the tsar'. Proudhon may not have been guilty of any greater nationalist bias than Marx himself; but whereas the latter is supremely aware of the immediate political implications of his position, Proudhon seems more interested in extending his principles to logical (though not always consistent) conclusions. Despite the difficulties Proudhon's distrust of nationalist movements created for him, in retrospect his emphasis on the dangers of nationalism, which he said would promote autocracy internally and wars between nation States, seems more profound than the easy endorsement of nationalism by many liberals and radicals.

Proudhon's dislike of nationalism reflected his fear not only of any tendency to political centralization, but also of a trend towards centralization of economic power. Marx on the other hand insisted on the necessity of retaining that 'unity of great nations which, if originally brought about by political force, has now become a powerful coefficient of social production' (*Selected Works*, 293). In this view the nation State is one stage in that historical development which is creating the necessary conditions for socialism, as it promotes the progress of industrialization. Engels comments that 'by far the most important decree of the Commune instituted an organisation of large-scale industry and even of manufacture which was not only to be based on the association of the workers in each factory, but also to combine all these associations in one great union'—an organizational form which would have led to communism. Therefore 'the Commune was the grave of the Proudhon school of socialism' (*Selected Works*, 260).

Industrialization

If Marxist support for national unity is related to acceptance of the need for full and rapid industrialization, Proudhon's emphasis on regionalism is certainly consistent with his general preference for a peasant economy and mode of life. A key distinction between Marxism and anarchism is in their view of industrialization. This contrast is complicated however by the fact that anarchists are themselves divided. Anarchist attitudes to industrial development fall into broadly three categories: opposition to industry as a dehumanizing process; acceptance of it as a necessary means of creating social wealth; and a conditional willingness to use industrial techniques, combined with proposals for directing industrial growth so that it is compatible with decentralism, and maintains close links with agriculture. Tolstoy is the most extreme exponent of the first position. In his view factory work, and its concomitant division of labour, is the antithesis of the healthy labour of the peasant; and mass production is only necessary in a society corrupted by luxury. Tolstoy also dismisses the Socialist belief that when the workers have become masters of the means of production they will adopt the living standards enjoyed by the bourgeoisie. Workers freed from the economic compulsion to do the jobs demanded by modern industry would refuse to be enslaved to machines, and would only accept a division of labour which produced obvious communal advantages. Abolition of wage slavery, like the abolition of serfdom, might require the loss of certain economic and cultural refinements now enjoyed by a few (see 'The Slavery of Our Times' in *Essays from Tula*).

Proudhon seeks to promote an anarchism based on an independent peasantry and small family workshops, whilst accepting the need for large-scale industry, which is to be owned and run by workers co-operatives. Both agrarian independence and industrial co-operatives are to be promoted by economic measures: virtually free credit leading to free competition; and a system of mutual exchange, designed to eliminate the middlemen between producers and consumers, based on use of labour cheques. A Peoples' Bank was the institution he hoped could promote both. He tried to inaugurate such a Bank in 1849, which was closed down for political reasons before its economic viability could be tested. Marx commented on Proudhon's ideas in a letter to J. B. Schweitzer (24 January, 1865):

> Proudhon's discovery of 'Credit gratuit' and the 'banque de peuple' based upon it, were his last economic 'deeds' . . . That under certain economic and political conditions the credit system can serve to hasten the emancipation of the working class . . . is quite unquestionable, self evident. But to regard *interest-bearing capital* as the *main form of capital* while trying to use a special form of credit, the alleged abolition of interest, as a basis for a transformation of society, is a thoroughly *petty-bourgeois* fantasy (*Selected Correspondence*, 190–1).

This critique is not entirely fair, since Proudhon did recognize the need for some social reforms—for example, redistribution of land by the local communes. Proudhon's writings do, however, convey a tendency to rely on economic formulas. These had some influence in America, where social conditions encouraged a demand for free credit. But his main legacy to the anarchist movement has been his emphasis on bypassing the political process, and concentrating on the independent economic action of the workers.

Proudhon has also helped to promote a tradition of positive support for agricultural as opposed to industrial values. Herbert Read writing almost a century later confesses :

> I am by birth and tradition a peasant . . . I despise this foul industrial epoch—not only the plutocracy which it has raised to power, but also the industrial proletariat which it has drained from the land and proliferated in hovels of indifferent brick (*Anarchy and Order*, 58–9).

Industrialization must, however, be endured in an attempt to get to the other side, when man can 'return to the land not as a peasant but as a lord'. Elsewhere Read stresses that it is retrogressive to forsake the inventions of modern technology, like the areoplane and the telegraph, and that 'liberty is always relative to man's control over natural forces'. As a result he endorses without qualifications anarcho-syndicalism. The syndicalist is for Read 'the anarchist in his practical rather than his theoretical activity'. The syndicalist answer to the organization of the economy and administration of society is summarized as follows :

> The syndicalist . . . proposes to liquidate the bureacracy first by federal devolution. Thereby he destroys the idealistic concept of the State . . . He next destroys the money monopoly and the superstitious structure of the gold standard, and substitutes a medium of exchange based on the productive capacity of the country—so many units of exchange for so many units of production. He then hands over to the syndicates all other administrative functions—fixing of prices, transport, and distribution, health and education. In this manner the State begins to wither away (*Anarchy and Order*, 101).

This picture owes a good deal to Proudhon, whose co-operatives foreshadowed the later concept of trade union control, and who had already in 1851 envisaged a similar role for professional associations when suggesting that education should be organized directly by parents and teachers. Proudhon assumed however an administrative function for the local communes, though he does not suggest a detailed geographical administrative system until his later, and less anarchist, work on *The Federative Principle*. The role of the local community in relation to industrial organization has been one of the issues tending to divide anarchists and syndicalists.

Bakunin and Malatesta represent that wing of anarchism which unhesitatingly accepts industrialism and technology. Malatesta takes

for granted the need for division of labour and the technical direction of collective undertakings on a large scale. He also favours in
principle international control of crucial raw materials (coal, minerals,
oil), but urges that in practice a country which achieved a socialist
revolution would have to become self-sufficient, or do without these
raw materials, until socialism was established everywhere. Bakunin's
commitment to propogate anarchism among the peasants of Italy and
Spain has meant that his anarchism is associated more closely with
the peasant commune than the industrial collective (see, for example,
Gerald Brenan, *The Spanish Labyrinth*, chapter VII on 'The Anarchist', which emphasizes this element in Bakunin's approach exclusively). Nevertheless, Bakunin fully endorsed Marx's economic
theory and Marx's belief in increasing world economic interdepend-
ence. Daniel Guérin, writing on anarchism from a syndicalist standpoint, concludes his recent book *L'Anarchisme* as follows :

> Constructive anarchism, which found its most accomplished
> expression in the writings of Bakunin, relies on organization,
> self-discipline, integration, a centralisation which is not coercive
> but federal. It depends on large-scale modern industry, on modern
> technology, on the modern proletariat, on internationalism on a
> world scale (181).

Bakunin contrasts economic and political centralization. In Switzerland, for example, the increase in political centralization after 1848
produced no progress except in the economic domain : 'like the
introduction of a single currency, a single standard of weights and
measures, large scale public works, commercial treaties, etc.' (*The
Political Philosophy of Bakunin*, 256). He denies that economic and
political centralization are inseparable. 'Economic centralization, the
essential condition of civilization, creates liberty; but political centralization kills it' (ibid.).

Other anarchists, however, have believed that local autonomy
requires economic devolution. Kropotkin's *Fields, Factories and
Workshops* is a detailed attempt to describe a decentralist use of
modern technology suitable to an anarchist ideal of society. He seeks
to combine craftsmanship with the benefits of scientific invention,
and to create organic links between industry and the land in order
to preserve rural values. He also aims to abolish excessive division of
labour—between individual workers, and between regions and
countries specializing in one type of industry or agriculture. The
idea is :

> Each nation her own agriculturalist and manufacturer; each
> individual working in the field and in some industrial art; each

individual combining scientific knowledge with the knowledge of a handicraft—such is, we affirm, the present tendency of civilised nations (6).

Small industries can use new technical developments to reduce manual labour and increase the output and quality of goods. Kropotkin suggests that the main advantages of large-scale industry are not in the application of technology but in the command big organization have over the market, both in purchasing raw materials and in securing outlets for their goods. While certain industries like iron works and mining enterprises require hundreds, or thousands, of workers to be on one spot, many factories either comprise several distinct industries under common management, or are 'mere agglomerations of hundreds of copies of the very same machine' (179). There are very few *technical* reasons why the machines should not be distributed between several establishments, or why the different processes of production should not be separated. Kropotkin also urges the potentialities of applying science to agriculture in order to increase production and cut down the time needed on agricultural labour. He backs up his prescriptions for an economy founded less on the division than the 'integration' of labour with an analysis of how far industrial technology is promoting new handicrafts and petty trades.

Technically and economically Kropotkin's research and specific proposals have naturally become outdated, a fact which leads Herbert Read (though in an introduction to Kropotkin's writings he suggests the details only require updating) to opt for industrial syndicalism. But other anarchists have insisted on the continuing relevance of Kropotkin's approach. Alexander Berkman stresses in his *ABC of Anarchism*, written in 1929, the importance of economic independence through self-sufficiency, citing the early experience of the Bolshevik Government trying to secure foreign capital. He also sees value in internal decentralization of industrial and agricultural organization if there were attempts to destroy the revolution by economic pressure. For the same reason Berkman deplores any attempt to suppress existing small-scale industries or home manufacturers. But his main reason for favouring such devolution is his estimation of its long term social effects in promoting contact 'between the farm and the city' and a sense of community. He regrets that 'most people are still in the thraldom of the Marxian dogma that centralization is "more efficient and economical" '. Centralization not only degrades the worker to being a cog in the machine, but tends to concentrate the running of industry in the hands of a powerful bureaucracy (92).

Paul Goodman writing since the last War has been pointing in a direction similar to Kropotkin, to whose inspiration he pays tribute. While emphasizing the general trend towards centralization, and the disposition, when 'organization begins to creak' to 'enlarge it further by adding new bureaus and overseers', he suggests there are some examples of a contrary tendency :

> The management of a giant corporation—General Motors is the classic example—can shrewdly decide to delegate a measure of autonomy to its corporate parts, because more flexible enterprising is more profitable in the long run. Similarly, a huge physical plant can be geographically dispersed, and the management somewhat decentralized, to save on labour costs . . . (*People or Personnel*, 23).

Goodman is, however, more cautious than Kropotkin about the blessings of technical invention, and argues the need to make conscious choices about our use of technology. He quotes John Ullman, a scientist, to the effect that 'the invention of flight . . . is probably on balance a curse' (*Utopian Essays and Practical Proposals*, 27). Technical assumptions tend toward centralization, and so create inefficiency :

> For instance, it can be demonstrated that, except in highly automated factories where labour cost is small compared to fixed capital, or in heavy mining attached to its site, for the most part large scale industrial plants and concentrations of industry are less efficient than smaller ones that assemble parts machined in small shops; it is cheaper to transport the parts than the workers (*Utopian Essays*, 30–31).

As unit cost of production falls, so the unit cost of distribution rises; thus 'it is likely that much of the vast technology of food processing and transportation is inefficient'. Goodman points out also that in an age of machines most people have no notion of how they work, so 'the mass of people are in bondage to a system of service men for even trivial repairs' (32). Goodman is not against all centralization. He suggests that in certain areas where there are no district limits but something must be done—for instance smog control, or rapid decisions must be taken—for example air traffic control, or where there is a temporary emergency, central authority is necessary. There are also gains, as Bakunin saw, in central decision on standardization of currency or weights and measures. Indeed Goodman suggests that in certain areas, like standardized building materials or spare parts, more 'centralization' is required (*People or Personnel*, 9–11). Nor is he urging efficiency as a key criterion : 'A more human-scaled production has obvious political and cultural advantages; it allows for more flexible planning, it is more conducive to scientific education and invention' (*Utopian Essays*, 32).

Goodman is speaking of a situation in which technological criteria are related to a particular type of profit-motivated economy, in a country where there is (despite areas of extreme poverty) an unprecedented degree of affluence. He comments, for example, on 'the tendency of the manufacturers to build obsolescence and nonrepairability into the machinery'. Though American society may be seen as a warning against uncritical pursuit of industrialization and its latest technology, a critique of the life style of a society moving into the automation age has little direct relevance to countries struggling for a subsistence level standard of living for their people, many of whom have not moved into the bicycle age. But there are a few groups in the Third World which favour a Kropotkin-style approach to economic growth, the most obvious example being the Gandhian movement in India. Gandhi himself always linked his political agitation for Indian independence to a constructive programme for building up economic independence, and promoting village crafts like weaving to combat dependence on English produced cottons. His approach was not unlike Berkman's: a practical sense of the requirements of revolutionary change, and a profound belief in the values of local community. Since Indian society, like Russia in the nineteenth century, rested primarily on the great mass of peasants living in semi-feudal conditions in the villages, Gandhi, like Tolstoy, looked to the tradition of the village commune, laid most stress on handicrafts as a form of self-help, and, like Tolstoy, saw a partial solution to poverty in voluntary abstinence. (This view was encouraged by his personal ascetiscism, which, also like Tolstoy, but more realistically, he adopted both for its moral virtues, and as a means of identification with the poorest peasants.) Gandhi's views on industrialization were ambiguous, and are open to varying interpretation, but he tended to differ from Tolstoy in welcoming industry and technology, provided they were socially applied to ease human labour, but not to throw the masses out of work; and were adopted on a human scale compatible with decentralist political democracy.

One Marxist criticism of the Gandhian approach is that it misunderstands the requirements of economic development. A Hungarian economist discussing Gandhi's ideas comments that Gandhi's 'dislike of modern technology and industry and his bias against towns' are mistaken, as industry is indispensable in every developing country, and 'wherever there is industry urbanization will be inevitable' (*The New Hungarian Quarterly*, No. 37, Spring 1970, 170). But Professor Bognár concedes that Gandhi was partially right: traditional technology, especially in India where there is an enormous surplus of labour, will be needed for generations; and rapid increase in agricultural output is vital to stave off famine, so 'the weight of agriculture is substantially larger than was assumed in traditional "pro-industry" economic theories'. Finally, Gandhi's belief that 'recurring gaps in the balance of the economic development of society' could be bridged by reducing consumption (as well as expanding production) though it 'runs counter to the progress of human society and the economy' nevertheless makes some sense in a poor, densely populated, country with a high birth rate.

The City versus the Country

Conflicting attitudes to large scale industry are closely related to attitudes towards cities. Tolstoy totally rejects city life, which he sees as wantonly destructive of the beauties of nature, bad for peoples' health, and worse for their morals. *Resurrection* starts with this passage :

> Though men in their hundreds of thousands had tried their hardest
> to disfigure that little corner of the earth where they had crowded
> themselves together, paving the ground with stones so that
> nothing could grow . . . filling the air with the fumes of coal and
> gas, cutting down the trees and driving away every beast and every
> bird—spring, however, was still spring, even in the town (19).

Proudhon's peasant background and regional loyalty predisposed him to distrust the metropolitan culture of Paris. Paris, moreover, both symbolized and propagated the centralization of all branches of French life. As De Tocqueville wrote : 'Paris was becoming more and more the national arbiter of taste, sole centre of authority and of the arts, the focal point of all that was most vital in France . . .' (*The Old Régime*, 75). Proudhon is very aware that French Revolutions were too often both made and defeated in Paris. Rather than blaming the success of Caesarism in the 1850s on the conservatism of the peasants, he blames instead the political organization which allowed Paris to dominate France, and a political conception of democracy which enshrined this domination of the Provinces by a Paris-based Assembly. Kropotkin, on the other hand, combined respect for a peasant mode of life with an awareness of the liberating and cultural role of the medieval cities, which developed areas of self-government, promoted trade and prosperity, and encouraged technical and artistic skills. Kropotkin also responded eagerly to the Parisian revolutionary tradition from 1789–1871, and valued the radical consciousness it bred.

The implications of the debate about the values of rural versus city life have changed with the impact of modern technology and industry on both, and on society in general. Paul Goodman suggests that in our present era of regimentation and urban anomie, there is a good deal of validity in both 'a conservative and peasant critique of centralized court and town as inorganic, verbal and ritualistic' (Tolstoy), and 'a democratic urban critique of centralized bureaucracy and power . . .' (he puts both Proudhon and Kropotkin into this category). Goodman adds: 'We need to revive both peasant self-reliance and the democratic power of professional and technical guilds . . .' (_People or Personnel_, 12).

He is primarily concerned with revivifying these values within American cities. Together with Percival Goodman he has made detailed planning proposals for remedying some of the ills of New York and Manhattan—the housing shortage, blighted industrial areas and traffic-congested streets—whilst urging a degree of neighbourhood self-government in running schools, promoting urban renewal, and policing local areas. Specific proposals are, however, linked to a wider ideal for community planning and architecture. Form follows function. But is the _function_ good? Does it make sense, and does it make for beauty, what are its consequences? Only such ethical questions will provide the basis for adjusting means to ends of community planning (_Communitas_ 19).

Apart from accepting that growth of cities is inevitable, Marxist theory tends to be intrinsically more favourable to the values of city life. Marx's own attitude is diametrically opposed to Proudhon's peasant and rural bias. In the _Manifesto_ Marx saluted the Bourgeoisie for having 'rescued a considerable part of the population from the idiocy of rural life'. In his analysis of the _Eighteenth Brumaire of Louis Napoleon_, when he is explaining why the peasants do not strictly form a coherent class because of their isolation from each other, he compares them with overtones of contempt to 'a sack of potatoes'. On the other hand, Marx, and particularly Engels, were well aware of the horrors of industrial slums. If they made the connexion between city life and civilization denoted by the Latin word for city, (_civitas_), they also drew on the classical tradition in which cities were not only centres of culture and politics, but were (like the medieval cities) small in size, with the countryside easily accessible. Moreover, Marx recognized, at least in the abstract, that the gap between the city and the country was damaging to the inhabitants of both, and proposed in the _Manifesto_ that a Communist society would end the distinction between town and country.

Democracy and Egalitarianism

Diverging attitudes to the industrial and urban revolution are closely
connected with differing assessments of the era of 'democracy' ushered
in by the French Revolution. One of the overtones of the word
'democratic' has been willingness to identify with 'the people' or
'the masses', whom anti-democrats see as 'the mob' or the 'ignorant
multitude'. Proudhon's attitude is interestingly ambivalent, and not
altogether dissimilar from De Tocqueville's. The latter moves between
appreciation of the particular virtues of the spirit of democracy,
and reversion to an inborn sense of the superiority of aristocratic
values. Proudhon moves between acting as a socialist spokesman for
the wronged workers (even Marx commended his courage in adopting this role in 1848), and a positive disdain for the shiftless urban
proletariat. Proudhon seems to draw on the republican tradition in
which democracy is associated with urban mob rule, and the related
danger that the masses, lacking the education or the economic
independence to sustain civic liberty, will veer towards popular
despotism. Indeed, Proudhon argued in *The Federative Principle* that
historically the aristocracy and bourgeoisie have tended to protect
liberty and federalism, whilst the masses have supported a despotic
and unitary State. In *The General Idea of the Revolution in the
Nineteenth Century* he comments that if he accepted totally the
innate virtues of universal suffrage, he would have to support Louis
Napoleon as the choice of the people. Proudhon draws the conclusion that the people are by circumstance objectively better placed to
support liberty wholeheartedly than are the bourgeoisie, who spon-
sor liberalism, but necessarily rely on an exploitative economic and
political system. But the people as a whole must be protected from
their own folly by a federal structure which limits the effects of
their mistakes. Complementary to this analysis Proudhon stresses
the inherent defects in universal suffrage and the referendum, which
rest on the fallacy of the collective will, and in practice will result in
manipulation from the top.

Proudhon's attitudes tend to be reflected by Herbert Read, who
can also display contempt for the majority of the people. 'Such a
majority, as any intelligence test will immediately reveal, is inevitably an ignorant majority . . .' (*Anarchy and Order*, 15). Read
recognizes this attitude leads towards élitist politics, and elsewhere
unhesitatingly endorses the need for genuine democratic participation in running society, while desiring to dispose of democratic
shibboleths like 'universal franchise' which is 'no more essential to
democracy than divine right is to monarchy'.

The tone of Kropotkin is much more consistently democratic. He never wavers in his faith in the capacity of the people—not just in a future society, but here and now if they are given half a chance. Whereas Proudhon distrusts revolution which may unleash 'anarchy' in the perjorative sense, Kropotkin welcomes revolutions which liberate the suppressed capacity for self-organization :

> Give the people a free hand, and in ten days the food service will be conducted with admirable regularity. Only those who have never seen the people hard at work . . . can doubt it. Speak of the organizing genius of the 'Great Misunderstood', the people, to those who have seen it in Paris in the days of the barricades, or in London during the great dockers' strike, when half a million of starving folk had to be fed, and they will tell you how superior it is to the official ineptness of Bumbledom (*The Conquest of Bread*, 79).

This view is not altogether antagonistic to Proudhon's belief that men must acquire political experience in local organization—Kropotkin admits people may make serious mistakes in an electoral context, where they lack means or criteria for clear judgments. But Kropotkin is happy to take democratic risks—Proudhon's caution underlies his general scepticism about the wisdom of any attempt to seize political power.

Kropotkin's democratic and revolutionary optimism is echoed by Berkman and Malatesta, though the latter, who had a strong sense of the political difficulties which would be encountered after a revolution, criticized Kropotkin for radiating excessive optimism on the question of a speedy solution to the problem of economic scarcity. Nor is it surprising that a democratic commitment should be linked to the total economic egalitarianism of the communist anarchists. Proudhon, on the other hand, opposed complete equality in the economic sphere. He believed that private property was an incentive to hard work; he also wished individual talent and industry to be rewarded. In his proposed co-operatives all individuals would be given varied experience and equal opportunities; but skill and responsibility would earn higher salaries. Proudhon, like many nineteenth-century liberals, also feared that a communally imposed equality would lead to a loss of individual independence and liberty, and defended the rights of private property as a necessary bulwark of personal liberty. While recognizing State ownership of land might be preferable to the existing system of ownership, Proudhon attacks the dogma of 'association', and the principle of 'fraternity', as utopian goals hiding a despotic tendency to force humanity into conformity with principles repugnant to human nature.

Class Rule and Elites

Marx condemned Proudhon for his 'sham criticism' of utopias in which 'there is the anticipation and imaginative expression of a new world', and replacing this utopian communism by his own 'petty-bourgeois' utopia (*Selected Correspondence*, 223). Marx is much closer to the anarchist communists in his commitment to equality and fraternity as social values, in his hopes for revolution, and trust in popular action. But Marxism parts company with anarchism on two points of political importance. Though Marxism has generally adopted the democratic language of the French Revolution, it has equally insisted that 'the people' form distinct social classes, and that the immediate aim of the socialist revolution is the *class* rule of the workers. Marxism has also been prepared to accept the validity of universal suffrage as a basis for democratic government in a socialist society. 'The way out of parliamentarianism', commented Lenin, 'is not, of course, the abolition of representative institutions and the electoral principle, but the conversion of the representative institutions from talking shops into "working" bodies' (*The State and Revolution*, 79). These two issues are particularly significant for the organization of society during the transition period from socialism to true communism envisaged by Marx. Bakunin suggests that both the idea of class rule, and reliance on universal suffrage, enhance the dangers implicit in the Marxist theory that in the transition period it is necessary to retain the instruments of the State—this time a State governed by the majority class, the workers, and directed against the minority of the previous ruling class.

Bakunin is particularly wary of a theory of class rule which seeks to subordinate the peasantry to the workers: 'I do not believe that even under the most favourable circumstances the city workers will have sufficient power to impose communism or collectivism upon the peasants; and I have never wanted this way of realizing socialism, because I hate every system imposed by force' (*The Political Philosophy of Bakunin*, 400). When discussing what is meant by the 'dictatorship of the proletariat', Bakunin asks:

What does it mean: 'the proletariat raised into a ruling class'? Will the proletariat as a whole be at the head of the government? ... This dilemma is solved very simply in the Marxist theory. By a people's government they mean the governing of people by means of a small number of representatives elected by the people. Universal suffrage—the right of the whole people to elect its so-called representatives and rulers of the State—this is the last word of the Marxists as well as of the democratic school. And this is a falsehood behind which lurks the despotism of a governing minority . . . (287).

He comments that in response to the anarchists' polemic the Marxists had conceded that 'Anarchism or freedom is the goal, the State or dictatorship is the means.' However Bakunin maintains: 'No dictatorship can have any other aim but that of self-perpetuation.' Therefore, as soon as the workers capture the State, they ought to 'proceed with its destruction'. Yet according to Marx the people should strengthen the State, 'and transfer it in this form into the hands of its benefactors, guardians, and teachers, the chiefs of the Communist Party' (288).

Anarchists' early experience of the Bolshevik régime in Russia, where a number of prominent anarchist exiles had returned to participate in the building of socialism, tended to confirm their belief in Bakunin's critique. The symbol of their final disillusionment was the attack on Kronstadt in 1921, when Lenin and Trotsky turned the 'workers'' army against the dissident sailors and workers demanding free Soviets. Alexander Berkman noted:

March 7—Distant rumbling reaches my ears as I cross the Nevsky . . . Kronstadt has been attacked! Days of anguish and cannonading . . . The people on the streets look bowed with grief, bewildered . . .

March 17—Kronstadt has fallen today. Thousands of sailors and workers lie dead in its streets. Summary execution of prisoners and hostages continues.

March 18—The victors are celebrating the anniversary of the Commune . . .

(from *The Bolshevik Myth*. Extract in Horowitz, ed., *The Anarchists*, 506).

Both Berkman and Emma Goldman produced specific critiques of the early evolution of Soviet Socialism. Bakunin's style of analysis is, however, at a level of such generality that it could be applied equally to Russia in the 1920s, 1930s or 1960s. For Bakunin himself, engaged in a movement still far from reaching its goal, a degree of rhetorical generalization was inevitable. But there is a temptation inherent in this style of polemical anarchism to allow opposition to the abstraction of 'the State' to preclude concrete understanding of any particular régime. As a result important political differences are swept aside as peripheral. 'There is only one kind of freedom: total freedom', writes a contributor to *Anarchy*, 'it cannot exist within the framework of somebody's state, not though his name be Dubcek, nor Johnson nor Castro nor De Gaulle' (*Anarchy*, No. 94, December 1968, 383). Herbert Read commenting that in the course of the Civil War the Spanish Government had 'created, in the form of a standing army and a secret police, all the instruments of oppression', says therefore Franco's victory 'regrettable in that it leaves the power of the State in still more ruthless hands, is to be looked upon with a certain indifference . . .' (*Anarchy and Order*, 51–2).

One objection to Bakunin's denunciation of 'Marxism' is that it is positively misleading about Marx's own theory of the State. In the *Manifesto* Marx had certainly envisaged State control of credit, transport and communications, industry and land. The proletariat will after winning political supremacy 'centralise all instruments of production in the hands of the State, i.e. of the proletariat organized as the ruling class' (*Selected Works*, 52). The definition of 'the State' here is sufficiently ambiguous to suggest the authoritarianism Bakunin detected. But Marx's overall position is anti-statist in emphasis. In his early writings he regarded the State as one aspect of alienation; and in his later years he attacked Lasalle's attempt to woo support from Bismarck's State, and was scathing about the slogan of the 'free state' adopted in the 1875 German Social Democrats' Gotha Programme. His pamphlet on the Commune, which he describes as 'the political form at last discovered under which to work out the economical emancipation of Labour' suggests no predisposition to impose a political form on a workers revolution, and indicates a far from authoritarian view of the 'dictatorship' of the proletariat.

Indeed, it is interesting to note that whereas there are considerable differences between Marx and Proudhon, Bakunin is very close to Marx on many issues. For example Bakunin too maintains that what the Commune wanted 'was not the dissolution of the national unity of France but its resurrection'. This unity is the antithesis of a bureaucratic State régime. Where Bakunin differs is insisting such unity must be 'federalist' in character (see *The Political Philosophy of Bakunin*, 272). Lenin basing himself on Marx speaks of 'voluntary centralism' and 'the voluntary amalgamation of the communes into a nation', which is not to be confused with a bureaucratic and military centralism imposed from above (*The State and Revolution*, 91–2). It is by no means clear how this differs from Bakunin's own programme of spontaneous federation, since in both formulations the organizational implications are vague. Max Nomad argues in *Apostles of Revolution* that Bakunin used libertarian slogans primarily as a politically useful tactic in his struggle against Marx's leadership of the First International. Nomad stresses Bakunin's own predisposition to rely on a revolutionary élite to act as a vanguard, and suggests that Bakunin was foreshadowing organizational tactics later adopted by Lenin. Nomad's thesis is highly polemical and certainly questionable. He assumes that the existence of a conscious revolutionary minority must necessarily mean a dominant élite seizing power after a revolution. He also links Lenin and Stalin indiscriminately as Bakunin's unwitting heirs. But Nomad does usefully underline that Marxists and anarchists in the nineteenth century faced common problems of how to put their ideals into practice, that anarchism has remained primarily a doctrine of those in opposition, and that anarchist awareness of the traps of political power is no guarantee that they could avoid them. Indeed Nomad's description of Makhno's career suggests that in some circumstances they could not.

Leaving aside the question of adapting ideals to political realities, it is relevant that the Marxist ideal of a workers' democracy does diverge significantly from the anarchist communist ideal, exemplified by Kropotkin's comments on the Paris Commune. Kropotkin sees the Commune's adherence to the principle of government not as an illustration of the political realism of the workers engaged in a concrete experiment in socialist organization, but as a sign of lingering prejudice in favour of the institutions of the old society.

> In the midst of the Commune the ancient principle of authority cropped up and the people gave themselves a Council of the Commune, on the model of municipal Council's elsewhere. And yet if we admit that a Central Government to regulate the relations of Communes between themselves is quite needless, why should we admit the necessity to regulate the mutual relations of the groups which make up each Commune? (*The Commune of Paris*, 10).

Kropotkin is opposing any form of representative government, and relying solely on the free initiative of 'groups' and on the spontaneous inventiveness of individuals.

Social Administration without Government

As a comment on the best way of running a revolution Kropotkin's views are pertinent. There is ample evidence of practical improvization to deal with immediate crises, and the liberating effect a revolution may have on men's imaginations. Kropotkin's most persuasive criticism of the Commune's city government is that it stultified its own goals:

Paris sent her devoted sons to the Town Hall. There, shelved in
the midst of files and old papers, obliged to rule where their
instincts prompted them to be and do amongst the people, obliged
to discuss where it was needful to act, and to compromise where
no compromise was the best policy; . . . they saw themselves
reduced to impotence. Being paralysed by their separation from
the people . . . they themselves paralysed the popular initiative
(10).

Certain parallels exist between Kropotkin's observations on the
Commune's government and the more or less irrelevant role played
by the Spanish Government during the real military and social
struggles of the Civil War. Anarchists can indeed point to numerous
instances in which an official leadership tied to orthodox procedures
of political organization, and to conventional concepts of political
realism, have slowed down or betrayed a popular struggle. But it is
far from certain that the total informality of organization proposed
by Kropotkin is appropriate to dealing with long term problems of
economic co-ordination, or that the degree of activism and involvement typical of revolution can be expected from people in day to
day life, or that it is even to be welcomed as an ideal.

It is implicit in Kropotkin's approach here that not only the State
machine will wither away, but all forms of governmental organization. If what government means is an administrative structure, then
both federalist and syndicalist proposals clearly involve formal organization. If Kropotkin's *ad hoc* co-operation between groups within a
commune were to continue it would certainly evolve into organizational routines—though the way it had evolved might well affect
its degree of flexibility and freedom from authoritarianism. But
'government' has other connotations—of an 'authority' which may
resort to force. Government in this sense is closely connected to the
law—both depending ultimately on police enforcement, but claiming to embody social values and aims, and maintained by the passive
assent of the majority. If anarchists differ about details of economic
and administrative organization, they are unanimous in declaring
for the abolition of law and the police. The underlying theoretical
model which leads them to this conclusion is not however always the
same. There are at least three social models in which natural harmony
supersedes imposed and distorting forms of 'order': the reign of
economics, in which a hidden hand will promote a natural coin-
cidence of interests; the reign of reason in accordance with natural
law or historical evolution; and the traditional community exemplified by peasant villages or tribal organization.

The importance of economics dominated much nineteenth-century thinking. The fascination of the new science, and the evidence that economic activity involved a multiplicity of operations which could not be fully comprehended by a single intelligence, and which could therefore be harmed by conscious regulation, contributed to the idea of self-regulating economic harmony. So did the impact of early industrialization and technology, which seemed to point to the potentiality of unlimited wealth. They also seemed to be creating conditions in which men became necessarily dependent upon one another, and so could be brought to follow their natural economic interests by voluntary co-ordination. The first vision owes much to Adam Smith, the second to Saint-Simon, who recognized the need for conscious planning, but believed the 'administration of things', in accordance with scientific principles, would replace the 'government of men' by the arbitary will of other men. Proudhon seems to draw on both images. The State will be dissolved into Society, according to Proudhon, when industrial division of labour supersedes class divisions; when the collective force of workers' co-operatives replaces that of government armies; when commerce promotes the replacement of law by contract; when 'centralization' of interests through credit takes the place of obedience to central power; and through free competition, equality of exchange, and equilibrium of values and properties.

The implicit natural law basis of anarchism has been developed in accordance with three different strands in political theory; belief in enlightened rationalism, in historical teleology, and in science as a guide to social action. For Godwin moral principles are accessible to the reason of all right-thinking men and are self-evident truths which will constrain men to accept their conclusions with a kind of mathematical rigour. Bakunin also appealed to the moral conscience of mankind but was influenced by Hegelianism towards a view of history in which human consciousness develops through a necessary dialectic with social reality towards a true moral understanding. Bakunin's faith in reason is also supplemented by a sense of the diversity of society : the Adam Smith view of economics is broadened into a general view of the complexity of social activity, which cannot without repression be fitted into the mould of any governmental design. Bakunin argues that no individual or group can devise a social organization capable of satisfying the multiple and diverse interests, aspirations, and needs of the people. 'Such an organization would ever be a procrustean bed into which violence, more or less sanctioned by the State, would force the unfortunate society' (The Political Philosophy of Bakunin, 299). Therefore, only popular spontaneous organization is likely to realize this diversity and satisfy real interests and needs.

Kropotkin elaborated the view that anarchism is based on the
scientific study of society and natural history and so a rational
attempt to live in harmony with natural and social 'laws'. He
pointed to the role of natural instincts in creating a morality of
sympathy between men, and to the role of tradition and social habit
in creating a set of largely unquestioned beliefs which guide man's
behaviour. For Kropotkin tradition and habit are analogous to the
instinctual behaviour patterns of animals, and historical evolution
parallels natural evolution. His moral views conflict with those of
Godwin, who lays great stress on scrupulous rational calculation of
the path of duty. Kropotkin stresses rather the role of natural instinct
(for example, to protect a child), spontaneous sympathy, and the in-
spirational force of heroic or devoted actions, which society turns into
legends and teaches its children.

Kropotkin's approach was strongly influenced by the concrete
examples of the peasant communes, or the Siberian tribal communities, with their own customs and values. The importance of this
model is even clearer in Tolstoy when he comes to talk about what
will replace organized forms of law and punishment. The economic
solution suggests that crime will disappear when individual interests
are satisfied—it has no built-in answer as to how intermediate difficulties should be met. The solution based on natural reason or conscience assumes crime is an error which reason and social progress
can remedy, and in the interim the answer is moral suasion and the
coercion of public opinion—to which Godwin explicitly appeals. But
the solution based on examples of previous or existing communities
incorporates concrete procedures. Tolstoy comments:

> Why suppose that there cannot be tribunals without violence?
> Trial, by people trusted by the disputants, has always existed and
> will exist, and needs no violence ... Russian communes migrating
> to distant regions, where our Government leaves them alone,
> arrange their own taxation, administration, tribunals, and police,
> and always prosper until government violence interferes (*Essays
> from Tula*, 116).

The Administration of Justice

Proudhon also looks to the past for his practical proposals about the
administration of justice in his book on *The General Idea of the
Revolution in the Nineteenth Century*, but focuses on the history
and theoretical development of the legal tradition itself. A distinction
can be made between law which involves restitution for a wrong,

broadly the category of civil law; and law which involves punitive retribution, penal law. Durkheim discussed this distinction, but considered that punishment expressing the moral reprobation of the community was a necessary aspect of social cohesion; and that the moral norms of any society would always tend to be so constricting that they would promote individual defiance and rebellion. Proudhon, however, uses this distinction to argue that the concept of reparation (to individuals or to society) should be extended to the realm of penal law to eliminate entirely the idea of vengeance. A second and related distinction is between arbitration—neutral mediation between conflicting parties who agree to accept the arbiter's decision, and the judgment of legal courts representing imposed authority. Proudhon seeks to replace judges by arbiters who will be elected by both parties to a case.

Proudhon's suggestions have precedents in primitive law, which as De Jouvenel comments 'could do without means of coercion. Judgment was an arbitral award accepted in advance. Maine noted the entire absence of sanctions in the earliest systems of Law' (*Power*, 275–6). Kropotkin stresses in his pamphlet on *The State* that common law or customary law provides a greater protection for individuals and greater independence for communities. 'Customary law naturally pertains to local life and Roman law to centralisation of power' (35). Kropotkin draw on Maine's *Ancient Law* to describe how justice was understood and administered in tribal and village communities, and adds :

> all notions of right which we find in our codes (mutilated to the advantage of minorities), and all forms of judicial procedure, in so far as they offer guarantees to the individual, had their origin in the village community. Thus, when we imagine we have made great progress—in introducing the jury for example—we have only returned to the institution of the barbarians, after having modified it to the advantage of the ruling classes (15).

Kropotkin wished to restore the unity between social attitudes and the administration of justice that existed under customary law, by eliminating formal legal codes, which tend to perpetuate a rigid class structure based on legal distinctions, and to crystallize social institutions and attitudes long after society itself has begun to change. Kropotkin's point can be amply illustrated from English law—for example, the heavy sentences attached to crimes against property, the long campaign required to alter legislation on homosexuality, and the perpetuation on the statute books of crudely drafted legislation like the Official Secrets Act of 1911 (whose repressive potentialities aroused concern early in 1970).

But it is clearly impossible simply to transpose a model of administering justice appropriate to a small, traditional and tightly knit community to a large, mobile and anonymous urban population. And it is even less possible to rely, as Godwin and Proudhon suggest, on the application of general principles of justice, dispensing both with formally defined rules of law and with formal procedures for administering them. Informal justice presupposes an agreement on moral and judicial principles, and their procedural application, unlikely except in a society with the cohesion and tradition which rationalism tends to destroy. Similar problems arise in relation to Kropotkin's desire to create a more flexible set of legal rules amenable to social change. Unless one can assume social homogeneity there may be passionately held divisions on issues of moral and social conduct and appropriate penalties. Moreover, Kropotkin is taking for granted a steady 'progression' in public opinion, whereas recent experience in Britain suggests that 'progressive' legal and penal reforms are supported only by a minority. Indeed, one strong argument in favour of legislation in areas like racial, religious or sexual discrimination is that the existence of laws carrying the weight of legal authority will influence public opinion in an egalitarian direction.

Nevertheless, it is interesting to notice that modern theories of penal reform tend to agree with nineteenth-century anarchist writers who criticized not only the barbarity of existing modes of punishment, but their social effects and their relevance in preventing crime. Considerable doubt has now been cast both on the idea of punishment as a form of social retribution and on the uses of punishment as a deterrent. Whilst there is a new danger, as anarchists have noticed, that modern psychology and sociology will be used simply as a more subtle instrument for manipulating 'social deviants', experiments in penal reform and developments in psychological theory do hold out possibilities of alternatives to the present penal system. Similarly there are areas of modern law—for example, legislation to prevent discrimination—in which law is used in a more flexible and less punitive manner, with a greater emphasis on arbitration, and a greater reliance on individuals and local communities to make the law effective. Despite anomalies involved in drafting and implementing this type of law it provides a model which might be extended. Whether judicial 'arbitration' between individuals is, as Proudhon suggested, appropriate to crimes like violent assault is more questionable. Kropotkin in his account of village justice in fact suggests that the village commune made a collective 'judgment' when finding the appropriate sentence for a crime under customary law.

Anarchists concerned to promote a more flexible, socially realistic and humane administration of law tend to look to the local community both as the unit in which a wide range of laws should be implemented, and as the unit in which any enforcement necessary should be carried out. Proudhon urged that every workshop, corporation, commune and locality should organize its own police just as it should organize its more general administration. Kropotkin recognizing that the family unit which used to bind its members together in a community of welfare is disintegrating, looks to new geographical and economic communities to play a similar role in dealing with 'moral' as well as 'material' troubles, for instance looking after 'criminals'. Paul Goodman suggests that in America the violence of modern urban police, and their ineffectiveness in preventing crime, points to the need for smaller units within cities to run their own police—a proposal which makes obvious sense for ghetto communities.

Utopian Thinking and Historical Progress

Anarchists tend to vary between making specific, gradualistic proposals in areas like police and penal reform, and upholding a radical and absolute demand for abolishing existing courts, jails and police forces. The former is more immediately relevant, and more likely to win converts among non-anarchists. But uncompromising radicalism can be justified at three levels. Without a 'utopian' commitment to question the underlying assumptions of social practices, proposals for reform tend to bypass the central problems, and may ameliorate a situation which ought never to be tolerated. Secondly, as Kropotkin indicates when discussing nineteenth-century changes in the treatment of the insane, there is often historical evidence that what seems 'utopian' to one generation is accepted as obvious good sense by their successors. Oscar Wilde commented that 'A map of the world that does not include Utopia is not worth even glancing at, for it leaves out the one country at which Humanity is always landing . . . Progress is the realization of Utopias' (*The Soul of Man under Socialism*, 43). Thirdly, as Kropotkin also emphasized, most people are prisoners of their own education, and of the reigning conventional wisdom. So their world view shuts out large stretches of historical experience, alien areas of social reality, and a vision of future possibilities. De Tocqueville, the least utopian of theorists, recognized the significance of this social blindness. He wrote of the mid-eighteenth-century French 'Physiocrats':

> It is a curious fact that when they envisaged all the social and adminstrative reforms subsequently carried out by our

revolutionaries, the idea of free institutions never crossed their
minds ... political liberty in the full sense of the term was
something that passed their imagination or was promptly dismissed
from their thoughts if by any chance the idea of it occurred to
them (*The Old Régime*, 159).

Marxism also retains a utopian dimension, which it inherits from
the historical optimism of the nineteenth century, and which is
intrinsic to any revolutionary political movement. But Marxism lays
much greater stress on the requirements of political and sociological
realism, which demarcate the boundaries of utopian possibility. 'Men
make their own history, but they do not make it just as they please;
they do not make it under circumstances chosen by themselves, but
under circumstances directly encountered and transmitted from the
past' ('The Eighteenth Brumaire of Louis Bonaparte', *Selected Works*,
97). Marxists accept the need for institutionalized systems of law and
government in any foreseeable socialist future. While Engels endorses
Saint-Simon's slogan that the government of men will give way to
the administration of things, he comments elsewhere in a highly
critical analysis of Bakunin that 'in this society there will above all
be no *authority*'. He adds 'how these people propose to run a factory,
operate a railway or steer a ship ... they do not of course tell us'
(*Selected Correspondence*, 336). Marx and Engels did envisage that
the socially repressive aspects of the State would fully disappear
when communism had been realized, but left the organizational forms
of such a society open. In all their specific statements about the
nature of a post-revolutionary socialist society they assume delegation of authority to government bodies, and a democratically organized system of law. Marx commenting on the Commune approved
the measures whereby magistrates and judges were to be 'elective, responsible, and revocable' and thus 'divested of that sham independence which has but served to mask their abject subserviency to all
succeeding governments ...' (*Selected Works*, 291–2).
    Ernest Barker has suggested that Marxism revived through Hegel
the Greek conception of politics, in which State and Society are not
distinguished, and that Marx wished to dissolve the State and re-
absorb its activities into Society. This suggestion is illuminating—
though Barker himself then confuses the issue by assuming Marx
equated 'society' with economic activity. Athens provides a rare
model of democratic and egalitarian government based on public
debate and the possibility of all citizens holding office: direct democracy may be seen as means of dissolving a separate State power into
Society. Athens also provides a model of law being operated in a
democratic and political mode, prosecutor and defendant pleading

their own case before a large jury of fellow citizens. The defects of this system of law, noted by constitutionalist theorists who prefer the classical model of Rome, spring from its democratic character.

Athens was not in any sense explicitly idealized by Marx and Engels It was, as Engels points out, based on slavery, degraded the status of women, and represented. in his analysis, the movement towards private property and centralized government power, in place of the equality, communalism and independence of the previous tribal societies. Moreover, a communism looking to the future was impatient of revolutionaries who dressed up in the clothes and symbols of antiquity. Engels regarded Athens as 'the prototype of the self-governing American municipality', but not a symbol of revolutionary possibilities. He concludes his study of the 'Origin of the Family, Private Property and the State' with a quotation from the anthropologist Lewis Morgan. The forthcoming society will be 'a revival, in a higher form, of the liberty, equality and fraternity of the ancient gentes' (*Selected Works*, 593).

It is, however, crucial to the Marxist approach that modern communism will be the product of an historically evolved social consciousness, drawing on the benefits of economic development and intellectual development, including a new understanding of the social powers which now appear to men as uncontrollable and alien forces. This understanding will enable men consciously to control social activity. The kind of culture and consciousness envisaged is not unlike the humanist confidence and creativity evolved in the Greek city state, but incorporating modern science and the much richer sense of individuality developed by bourgeois society. The conception of humanism which Marxism embodies stems both from the optimism of the French Revolution, which promulgated the universality of the 'rights of man', and from the influence of Hellenism on the German cultural renaissance around the beginning of the nineteenth century. Marx did, however, believe in his later writings that historical development had not only exacted a heavy price in the past, but that some price must be paid in the future. For example, the demands of industrialism must limit the free scope of the individual worker—a limit which automation may now transcend; or developing sophistication destroys certain kinds of art and culture.

The anarchist tendency to look to the medieval guild or township, or to present tribal or peasant societies, rather than to the evolution of existing trends, has by comparison both strengths and weaknesses. It avoids a facile optimism about 'progress', and the danger of identifying progress with technology; and it also challenges a crude historical determinism. But when Kropotkin, seeking to prove the possibility of 'harmony in an ever-changing and fugitive

equilibrium between a multitude of varied forces and influences'
(*Anarchism: Its Philosophy and Ideal*, 8), says this popular tendency
can be found in 'the clan, the village, the guild and even the urban
commune of the Middle Ages in their first stages', he is dodging
historical and sociological issues. Kropotkin bypasses the fact that
growth of individualism is usually associated with the breakdown
of medieval institutions, or the escape of the individual from the
clan. He also appeals to the rule of custom without examining its
possibly restrictive effects on individuality or the development of
intellectual culture. If an urban and industrial society is expected to
revert to the flexible rules of custom, in preference to formal law or
government of any kind, then the realism of this approach is questionable. If on the other hand one is aiming to avoid changing tribal
or peasant societies where these still exist, idealizing custom tends
to become conservative. Tolstoy recognizes that turning to the
village commune entails a rejection of urban and 'civilized' culture,
science and art. Proudhon is less willing to reject philosophy and
science. But like Tolstoy he accepts a peasant mode of living, including the patriarchal family as an ideal, which assigns women to their
permanent place in the home.

The Meaning of Politics

Even if one grants the possibility of forming new communities
endowed with a libertarian consciousness, an anarchist society which
avowedly relies on social control by a local community to replace
formal law and police is in danger, as George Orwell once pointed
out, of appealing to an extremely coercive public opinion. Moreover,
whatever the values of community by comparison with the anonymity and inhumanity of large cities, loss of anonymity may also
mean a serious loss of personal freedom. It is true that a genuine and
fairly stable community like a village may show more concern for
individuals, and more tolerance of eccentricity, than a larger society
governed by general codes and fashions; but its disapproval is also
more overwhelming, and even concern is not necessarily an unmixed
blessing.
    An anarchism which appeals primarily to the role of the local
community tends towards using the family as an attractive image
for social organization. The family has indeed always been a favoured
model—socialists overthrew the patriarchal image of the family which
justified paternal authority in government in favour of fraternal
equality. There are, however, difficulties in seeking to extend the
affection and personal understanding possible within a family circle

to a larger society—since the extension is either metaphorical or forced. This is true even of a society very small by modern standards, for example, classical Athens. Conscious deliberations about a society as a whole deal in categories of people and interests, and must exclude the unique personality and circumstances of each person affected by social decisions. Rousseau saw this gap between personal and communal interest, but resolved it in favour of public duty, whilst suggesting that ideally each person in his capacity as citizen would understand and agree the need to promote the 'general will' before his private needs or wishes. It is this impersonal aspect of judicial and political decisions and procedures that easily promotes inhumanity, that creates a gap between public and private morality, and arouses passionate protest against the artificialities of law and government. It is this sense that there is a separate realm of public affairs, which cannot be assimilated to other aspects of private life, which we inherit from the classical tradition, and which provides a primary definition of 'politics' (see Hannah Arendt, *The Human Condition*). Proudhon partially recognized the distinction between a private and public sphere when he urged the danger of trying to impose an artificial fraternity on society—but then appeared to deny politics in favour of economics.

It is possible, however, to see in Proudhon's espousal of economics a recognition of a basic distinction between a 'social principle' and a 'political principle'. The concept of economic activity can easily be extended to social activity—the identification of the two was not uncommon in the nineteenth century, and still dogs interpretations of Marxism. The German anarchist, Gustav Landauer, writing at the beginning of this century, drew a distinction between social and political action based on Proudhon's affirmation that social revolution was quite different from political revolution. Landauer's ideas are developed by his friend Martin Buber in an essay 'Society and the State' (reprinted in *Pointing the Way*). The difference between State and Society is the difference between two kinds of relationship and two modes of behaviour which have always coexisted, but have often not been distinguished. The social principle involves action by equals co-operating together, and is a principle of community. 'Political' action involves relationships of domination and subordination, and therefore the use of force, and is typical of the State. Buber goes on to suggest that political organization gives men at the top more power than they need to fulfil a specific function, and so they extend and consolidate this surplus of 'power'—a power which in reality stems from the social group as a whole.

The ambiguity of terminology, which confuses much political theorizing, is here revealed. Because the anarchist principle of 'social action' seems very close to the Greek conception of 'politics', realized most fully in direct democracy. Buber suggests that the Greeks confused the social and political sphere. This is misleading. While the *polis* comprised both the social and political community, the Greeks made a very clear distinction in principle between co-operative action between equals—'politics', and the relationship of force and domination epitomized by the rule of a master over slaves. In practice, however, politics of course tended to involve force and domination in various forms. The notion of 'politics' has by now come to include positive recognition of the necessity of force and coercion, of meeting 'power' with power, and of compromise with social realities in a very imperfect world—which is why anarchists reject 'politics', and Marxists, in the short term at least, do not.

4   Anarchism and the Individual

In the Introduction to this book a brief sketch of some better known anarchist thinkers and movements indicated the extreme diversity of the anarchist tradition. In the succeeding three chapters anarchist ideas have been contrasted with the individualist contract theory emanating from Hobbes; with the constitutional liberalism which find an important interpreter in De Tocqueville; and with the Marxist movement in socialist thought. These traditions are in themselves complex, but anarchism is in many respects much less coherent. Godwin's brand of anarchism can be seen as a logical extension of laissez-faire liberalism. But modern anarchists have frequently claimed to be the true heirs of the idealism and libertarianism of the utopian socialists and the early socialist movement; Bakunin and Malatesta, for example, are indisputably important figures in socialist history. And while at some levels anarchism seems further removed from constitutionalism, at others, as Proudhon in particular illustrates, there are common values and a common adherence to the republican heritage of political ideas.

In all these guises anarchism is a political doctrine—if one that displays a tendency to logical extremes and utopian commitment alien to the usual concept of what 'politics' is all about. There are, however, within the spectrum of anarchism elements which appear to stand right outside the normal political sphere and assert the primacy of non-political values—individualism, artistic creativity, moral commitment, romanticism, or simply the common pleasures of everyday living. But on examination these approaches all have relevance to any attempt to define the sphere of politics and the nature of political activity. In this chapter they are explored in relation to Hannah Arendt's attempt to set limits to the political realm; and their relevance for an anarchist theory of politics.

The Egoist

One thinker who has a recognized place in the evolution of anarchist ideas and attitudes, but who has so far scarcely been mentioned, is Max Stirner. He is perhaps the hardest thinker to understand, writing as he does in the context of Hegelianism in Germany in the 1840s; and the easiest to dismiss, since he leaves behind him no political movement, career as an activist, or independent claim to fame. Moreover, in summary (even by anarchists) his ideas can easily sound ridiculous, unattractive, or both. But Stirner, who can be seen as a forerunner of existentialism, does have certain very important things to say.

The central contention of *The Ego and His Own* is that for each individual the only universe that either does or *can* genuinely matter is his own. The individual's own life experience comprises all aspects of his being and personality—his sensuousness, his natural affections, his will to assert his own identity. This concrete individual is, however, always being sacrificed, and sacrificing himself, to abstractions and entities outside of himself. Most often the individual is sacrificed to the dictates of orthodox religion, or to that Moloch, the State. But Stirner is even more interested in exposing the abstractions of contemporary radicals, who also oppose Church and State, but seek to constrain the individual with the principles of liberalism or morality. He attacks too his contemporaries who have sought to end that form of alienation which arises when men deny their own highest attributes, and embody them in a God whom they worship, but have only succeeded in abasing the real individual before a new idol, the abstract essence of Man or Humanity (see Ludwig Feuerbach, *The Essence of Christianity*). This criticism is pertinent to that Marxist vision whose full richness is to be realized in the future, but which is often in danger of sacrificing to this end those men living and suffering here and now.

Stirner is precluded by his commitment to the pre-eminence of the individual self, distrust of intellectual abstractions, and belief that the future cannot be predicted in advance of experience, from systematic generalization of the social implications of his position. He is also perhaps more excited by iconoclasm. But he throws out certain illuminating ideas which have direct social relevance. He notices that fanaticism for an ideal for which a man is prepared to sacrifice himself may lead him to immolate others on the altar of this virtue —Stirner cites Robespierre. Secondly Stirner's 'egoism' does not exclude relationships with other people—it would indeed be an attenuated individuality which attempted to do so—but posits a spontaneous union between individuals, which is the antithesis of the formally imposed ties of 'society' (for Stirner 'society' has connotations of artificiality not, as for Kropotkin, of naturalness). This union is potentially subversive of a social order enforced by discipline. Stirner illustrates his point by looking at prisons:

That we *jointly* execute a job, run a machine, effectuate anything in general—for this a prison will indeed provide; but that I

forget that I am a prisoner, and engage in intercourse with you
who likewise disregard it, brings danger to the prison, and not
only cannot be caused by it, but must not even be permitted. For
this reason the saintly and moral-minded French chamber decides
to introduce solitary confinement, and other saints will do the
like in order to cut off 'demoralizing intercourse' (*The Ego and His
Own*, 218–9).

This passage is reminiscent of De Tocqueville's comments on how
a few warders could control all the prisoners in Sing Sing jail by the
device of isolating them from each other, and the implications of this
device for imposing political despotism. Stirner also has an almost
republican belief in the role of courage and sense of freedom. 'A
Nero is a "bad" man only in the eyes of the "good" . . . In old Rome
they would have put him to death instantly, would never have been
his slaves. But the contemporary "good" among the Romans opposed
to him only moral demands, not with their will' (54). And for Stirner
true 'freedom' cannot be given to a slave, but can only be won
through his own actions. Finally, he makes a distinction, which
Herbert Read takes up, between 'revolution'—which is an organized
political act; and 'insurrection'—which has political consequences but
is primarily 'a rising of individuals, a getting up without regard for
the arrangements that spring from it'. Insurrection is inspired by
'egoism', the desire to rise and exalt oneself.

The Artist

Herbert Read adopts this idea of spontaneous uprising because he
sees it as a way of escaping from the revolutionary trap—overthrow-
ing one power structure in order to replace it with another. But
insurrection may alter social attitudes, by 'creating a new morality
or new metaphysical values'. Read quotes Camus on the idea of
'rebellion' (which is close to Stirner's insurrection). Rebellion is for
Camus 'the refusal to be treated as an object and to be reduced to
simple historical terms. It is the affirmation of a nature common to
all men, which eludes the world of power' (*The Rebel*, 216). Read
goes on to argue that 'a power structure is the form taken by the
inhibition of creativity: the exercise of power is the denial of
spontaneity' (*Anarchy and Order*, 17). Read then translates Stirner's
insurrection into terms more social—he sees rebellion as an expression of unity and solidarity—and more idealistic: 'The slave is not
a man without possessions . . . but a man without qualities, a man
without ideals for which he is willing to die' (*Anarchy and Order*,
18).

It is the nature of ideals which especially interests Read. Ideals provide a utopian consciousness which may enable men to transcend the barriers of their existing social reality and promote historical change. Ideals may be dangerous partly because the imaginative conception of a utopia which is a totality may lead to authoritarian blueprints in which individuality is subordinated to the requirements of symmetry and order. But such ideals are necessarily creative constructs, and Read sees this elaboration of symbols as a primarily aesthetic activity, and 'the concretization and vitalization of ideals is one of the main tasks of the aesthetic activity in man' (20).

Therefore, the imaginative expression of social ideals is peculiarly the role of the artist. But it is far from being his exclusive role—the artist creates symbols which are 'as multiform as the feelings that motivate man', while social ideals only represent collective feelings. Where society is perverted by power the social ideals are also perverted, and the conditions for creating freedom eroded if not extinguished. In a corrupted society the artist faces an agonizing dilemma. He is cut off from the public he needs for his own creative work; and at the same time has a special and often dangerous responsibility to provide the creative impetus which may break down the barriers hemming in his society. In a very personal statement of why he had chosen to be an anarchist at a time, 1938, when the criterion of political responsibility might suggest the need for unconditional support of the democratic front against fascism, Herbert Read examines the possible ways in which artists may respond to the tensions of their position.

He cites Gauguin, who tried to escape from the commercialism of bourgeois society by going to Tahiti, only to discover that this paradise had been corrupted by particularly degraded representatives of bourgeois 'civilization'. In extremism an artist may escape by resorting to suicide, like the poet of the Russian Revolution, Vladimir Mayakovsky. In April 1930 Mayakovsky killed himself—Read quotes (62) the poem which Mayakovsky left behind him :

> As they say
> 'the incident is closed'.
> Love boat
> smashed against mores.
> I'm quits with life.
> No need itemizing
> mutual griefs,
> woes
> offences.
> Good luck and good-bye.

Read sees only one alternative to escape—he labels as escape retreat into isolation and private phantasy, which is destructive of art and of onself and that is: 'To reduce beliefs to fundamentals, to shed everything temporal and opportunist, and then to stay where you are and suffer if you must' (61).

The Moralist

Artists in Russia have frequently felt a social responsibility to rebel —among them Tolstoy, who also turned to anarchism. But Tolstoy found little social relevance in his art—except as a form of moral parable—and was prepared to renounce art in general together with all the other privileges and pastimes of aristocratic society. Tolstoy rejected culture in part as a nemanation of a society founded on exploitation, and so inherently 'false'. He was also aware of alternative values embedded in the peasants' own culture. Tolstoy's position as an artist and intellectual was naturally not as simple as this interpretation suggests, and was linked to his general ascetism and moral theory (for an interesting critical discussion, see George Orwell, 'Lear, Tolstoy and the Fool'). But his answer to his dilemma was a little like Gaugin's, in the sense that it was a flight towards simplicity, though in political terms Tolstoy stayed in Russia and defied both the censor and the police. To the degree that he was trying to escape he was doomed to failure. Georg Lukacs has suggested that the best novelists transcend their own explicit social doctrines because of their artistic commitment to reproduce the detail of social reality. As a result nowhere is 'Tolstoy's Christian plebeian dream of brotherhood with the peasants more powerfully refuted than in . . . *Resurrection*' (*Essays on Thomas Mann*, 16).

Tolstoy's attempt to identify with popular culture is, however, easier to grasp sympathetically than his pursuit of a moral purity based on a literal interpretation of the Christian gospels. Indeed, Tolstoy stands in opposition to many elements in the anarchist tradition. His emphasis on the need for sexual purity is from a Stirnerite standpoint a form of self-castration. Janko Lavrin suggests, in a generally critical assessment of Tolstoy's ideas, (*Tolstoy: an Approach*), that his efforts to achieve a generalized love of man purged of all sexuality may result in a form of peculiarly selfish domination, sacrificing others to one's own spiritual welfare. Lavrin refers to Prince Nekhlyudov in *Resurrection*, who is overcome by remorse when he recognizes, while sitting on a jury, that the defendant is a servant girl he once seduced. The Prince then tries to save her, and offers to marry her. Though Maslova is still attractive enough to turn every male head in the courtroom, the Prince now feels no flicker of sexual attraction, and, says Lavrin, no trace of spontaneous tenderness and generosity (Chapter IX, 'A Puritan's Progress'). The general point is implicit in Stirner, and can be elaborated from modern psychology. But Tolstoy's approach, which includes recognition of the inadequacy of the Prince's conversion, is as it is worked out in the novel both psychologically subtle and *socially* aware. It is clear from reading Tolstoy—even the contorted *Kreutzer Sonata*—that he rejects sex in part because of its degrading social usages (for a sympathetic defence of Tolstoy's general position, see R. V. Sampson, *Equality and Power*). He sees aristocratic young men taking peasant women out of momentary lust, or because it is the fashionable thing to do; powerful men displaying their ownership of beautiful women; mothers displaying their daughters in an attempt to make a good catch; women desperately cultivating the charms they know are their main weapon in establishing power over men. In *Resurrection* the Prince's realization that he has casually ruined Maslova's life is the first step in his progressive discovery of the realities of Russian society.

Most important of all, Tolstoy turns to the Gospels because he is, like Read, looking for a utopian vision and commitment, one which will shatter Tsarism and avoid the dangers of organized and violent revolution. In an essay discussing other anarchists, 'An Appeal to Social Reformers', Tolstoy comments that while they recognize the importance of spiritual weapons in abolishing power, they fail to provide the religious basis which is necessary to create this spiritual force. Nor do they realize that only a religious life-conception will enable men to live in an anarchist society and to co-operate without violence. This view has been largely borne out by experiments in 'community' living; Read notes after reading Infield's historical study of *Co-operative Communism at Work* that the most successful communities were religious or—as in the case of non-religious co-operative settlements in Palestine—drawn together by 'some central emotional impulse, comparable to the religious motive' (*Anarchy and Order*, 170). Berdyaev in a perceptive critique of Tolstoy recognizes the full significance of this religious element:

> The principle of non-resistance advocated by him aims at remaining
> within the realm of divinely created nature prior to, and
> independently of, any relations that might exist between the
> citizens of a state. It draws its force from those dimensions where
> the Law of God operates ever against the Law of the World, and it
> presents a challenge to man to return to those dimensions'
> (Introduction to *Essays from Tula*).

Tolstoy sees his gospel as one which has to be lived here and now. The answer to war is not peace conferences, but individual refusal to be conscripted or to co-operate with the war machine. The way to create anarchist society is not to await 'the revolution', but to start living it. That Tolstoy seriously tried to live up to this conception is a measure of his honesty. That the attempt could not fail to be incomplete and slightly absurd is due not only to the inherent difficulty of adopting a utopian stance in a 'realistic' and cynical world—a dilemma Read wryly accepts in calling himself an anarchist—but to the fact that Tolstoy, sophisticated in every sense of that word, chose as his ideal a peasant simplicity.

His instinct in linking his search for moral purity, asceticism, a sense of brotherhood and messianic vision to a peasant outlook was, however, in a way sound. Peasant societies may be able to fuse an idealistic and simple programme with religious fervour and pure faith. Gerald Brennan writes on rural anarchism in Andalusia in the late nineteenth century :

> 'The idea', as it was called, was carried from village to village by Anarchist 'apostles'. In the farm labourers' *gañanías* or barracks ... the apostles spoke on liberty and equality and justice to rapt listeners ... many learned to read, carried on anti-religious propaganda and ofter practised vegetarianism and teetotalism. Even tobacco and coffee were banned by some ... But the chief characteristic of Andalusian anarchism was its naïve millenarianism (*The Spanish Labyrinth*, 157).

The anarchists expected a new age in which even the landowners and the Civil Guard would be free and happy.

The Hero

Simple idealism may be linked either to fervent non-violence or to violent action. Idealistic violence as a form of peasant rebellion tends to be symbolized (and in due course sentimentalized) in the Robin Hood tradition of bandits as avengers of a robbed peasantry. This tradition merges via Bakuninist romanticism into the anarchist expropriators who robbed banks for the benefit of the revolutionary movement. Hobsbawm, in a recent book on the theme of *Bandits*, chooses as a symbol of the expropriators Francisco Sabaté from Barcelona. After the victory of Franco in the Civil War Sabaté was reduced to making brief raids into Spain from over the French border, and was eventually shot by the police. Sabaté's mode of life was simple, his habits were ascetic and he was always poor; and he acted with the conscious chivalry and daring of a hero, taking risks to avoid hurt to other people, and always walking *towards* the police. Hobsbawn quotes a comment by one of Sabaté's friends after his death: 'When we were young, and the Republic was founded, we were knightly though also spiritual . . . We have grown older, but not Sabaté . . . he was one of those Quixotes who come out of Spain' (106–7).

The image is attractive, but its quality depends on the character of the hero, and its validity depends on the social context. The danger of allying moral purism to exaltation of violence is that it can turn into the brand of fanatiscism which led in the Spanish Civil War to the murder of pimps and male prostitutes. While the peasant bandit transferred to the urban underworld tends to become a 'gangster'. If intellectuals espouse romantic violence they may blend quixotic righting of the wrongs of the poor with a republican tradition of public-spirited men who risk their lives to kill a tyrant. A good example was Alexander Berkman's attempt to shoot Frick, the man who during the Pennsylvania Homestead Steel Strike of 1892 imported the thugs who killed eleven strikers, including a ten year old child. But this style of action easily merges into more indiscriminate terrorism, or blends with ordinary criminality. French anarchists in the 1890s were confrointed with these dilemmas. Some of the French intellectuals at this time, many of whom inclined towards anarchism, adopted a dilettante pose towards violent deeds. When a homemade bomb was exploded in parliament a group of celebrities were asked by a journalist to comment, and one of them replied: 'What do the victims matter if the gesture is fine?' (Barbara W. Tuchman, 'Anarchism in France', in Horowitz, ed., *The Anarchists*, 452). This attitude veers towards that alliance between the intellectual élite and the underworld 'mob' that Hannah Arendt traces as one of the cultural strands leading towards fascism. At the other extreme rigorous intellectual consistency may take the form of idealizing merciless ruthlessness for the sake of the cause, and willingness to sacrifice to this end all moral scruples and individuals who get in the way. The fantasy of the ice cold conspirator, embodied in *The Catechism of a Revolutionist*, was played out with inflexible willpower by the Russian student Nechaev (responsible with Bakunin for the Catechism), who manipulated and cheated Bakunin, lied his way to revolutionary influence, murdered a fellow student who saw through him, and died defiant and unrepentant in a dungeon.

The Coward

The intellectual may, however, look for a solution in another form of popular experience, not to find a golden age simplicity, pure faith or romantic rebellion, but to discover a vein of commonsense and normality with which people protect themselves from the perils of politics. This emphasis on self preservation became one of the motifs in political thought at the time of the English Civil War. As noted in Chapter 1, not only is it central to Hobbes's brand of authoritarianism, but it took more subversive and anti-political forms. Irene Coltman in her book *Private Men and Public Causes* charting the various currents of thought emerging from the Civil War suggests that the insistence on self preservation had already found classic literary expression in Shakespeare's Falstaff. 'What is honour?', Falstaff asks himself just before a battle in which his main interest is to avoid being killed. 'Can honour set to a leg? No. Or an arm? No. Or take away the grief of a wound? No. Honour hath no skill in surgery, then? No. What is honour? A word . . . Who hath it? He that died o' Wednesday . . . Honour is a mere scutcheon' (*Henry IV*, Part I, Act V, Scene 1).

Falstaff's virtues are contrasted with the horrors of battle wreaked by men less prudently timid. They are also contrasted with opposing values. Shakespeare embodies in Hotspur, who would 'pluck bright honour from the pale-fac'd moon', the heroic virtues of ardent ambition, generosity and impetuous courage, which bring him to an untimely death at the hands of Prince Henry on the battle field. The Prince is more hard-headed and cold-blooded than Hotspur. He also knows when to renounce Falstaff's world and his personal friendship, which he does brutally on becoming King. Yet his sense of political realism is also a sense of responsibility, and is presented as being more conducive to the public good than Hotspur's gallantry or Falstaff's anarchy.

The Political Realm

Shakespeare tends to accept that rulers live in a separate sphere from their subjects, that their burdens are much greater and their decisions necessarily founded on necessity of state. This is the secular view of politics to be found in Machiavelli, which has since become an important influence on political theorizing. A sensitive modern interpretation which avoids crude Machiavellianism is to be found in Hannah Arendt's *The Human Condition*. She insists that certain values and attitudes are inappropriate to the political realm—among these, love, both personal love and universalized Christian love. This love 'can only become false and perverted when it is used for political purposes such as the change or salvation of the world' (47). This is a direct refutation of the Tolstoyan aspiration.

Hannah Arendt's position is based on a belief that there are separate realms of experience and activity, with different criteria applicable to them: religion, art, philosophy, and science—all distinct from the sphere of politics, as is the private world of the household. Given the confusions and dangers of trying to fit politics into the mould of another mode of understanding and experience, the idea of multiple spheres of activity is helpful. But any view which accepts a *total* separation of spheres runs into trouble. Their total separation within the experience of an individual implies the invasion of bureaucracy into the personality, Max Weber's 'parcelling-out of the soul'. Moreover, all these spheres must have a common locus in a given society, and their social separation is dangerous, since their *effects* cannot be totally separated. If science is pursued irrespective of social consequences, philosophy and art divorced from public relevance, religion concerned entirely with the other world, and if the average man retreats into his private life, the result may be pure Machiavellianism—rampant political irresponsibility. Total separation of spheres is potentially as disastrous as that Stalinism which, in a gross distortion of the Marxist attempt at social integration, dictated scientific and philosophical truth, decreed artistic forms, denied autonomy to moral standards, and invaded personal privacy.

When the Greek idea of politics as the public realm (located literally in the assembly place) is linked to the constitutional tradition, the picture that emerges is of a political sphere hedged round by distinct worlds over which politics may claim no dominion. The boundary between politics and private life protects individual freedom. The world of learning and of factual documentation creates, Hannah Arendt suggests, another boundary which resists political attempts to distort their truth. However, a constitutional outlook, formed under the necessity of setting up barriers to the incursions of royal power in a centralized State, tends to overlook the Greek understanding of the interpenetration of culture and politics; embodied for instance in the role of drama in refining the notion of justice, or in philosophical debates about moral and political concepts.

A modern defence of the interrelation between politics and other spheres can perhaps best appeal to a situation which is understood as the complete negation of free politics—'totalitarianism'. Hannah Arendt suggests in her study of *The Origins of Totalitarianism* that the logic of a total ideology excludes genuine thought: 'The self-coercive force of logicality is mobilized lest anybody ever start thinking—which as the freest and purest of all human activities is the very opposite of the compulsory process of deduction' (473). Thought in this sense is both spontaneous and creative, and so is capable of challenging the existing order and creating something new. The Polish philosopher Kolakowski says that creative thought is 'precisely the activity which cannot be duplicated by an automaton. Philosophy is the eternal effort to question all that is obvious . . . The police ideal of order is the order of a comprehensive file; philosophy's ideal is the order of an active imagination' (*Marxism and Beyond*, 40, 55).

Both the critical and the creative contributions of art and philosophy to society promote an ideal of individual and social freedom. The role of science is now peculiarly complicated, and in its impact on politics is frequently seen as a threat to freedom and creativity. This development is particularly ironical in view of the hopes placed in science as an instrument of enlightenment and liberation, though this identification of science with progress now helps perpetuate the dangers arising from superstitious respect for 'science'. in the natural sciences the aim of pursuing truth, and understanding the mysteries of nature, has been largely subordinated to the aim of using science to *dominate* nature. The prestige of natural science has led theorists for well over a century to attempt to create a social science of equal status, which would rid us of our present uncertainties. The triumph of this social science would appear to imply a total determinism, an uncovering of the 'laws' which individuals or societies must follow; but on the analogy of natural science it also involves use of this knowledge to direct and dominate society by the scientific élite. But this misconception of 'science' can be refuted from within the scientific tradition. Bakunin in one of his perceptive flashes argues in *God and the State* that the very nature of science—its tendency to generalization and abstraction—makes it unsuited to guide or govern a society. 'Science cannot conceive real individuals and interests' (60). Paul Goodman outlines in his essays on ' "Applied Science" and Superstition' (in *Utopian Essays and Practical Proposals*) the humanist inspiration of science, in which 'pursuit of natural truth is a transcending good' and in which the discipline of scientific habits is of positive value. When Kropotkin sought in *Modern Science and Anarchism* to relate anarchism to scientific method, his analogies with the animal world did not lead him to subordinate social experience to models drawn from the natural sciences. Instead he appeals to the evidence of history and anthropology, and popular experience. Anarchists stand within a tradition of science which seeks to pursue understanding for its own sake, but also applies this understanding to improve men's environment, and social conditions, in an experimental and critical way. From this standpoint 'sociology' or psychology may promote areas of freedom and creativity which seem to be denied by the iron necessities of power politics. Comfort for example sees modern sociology as upholding an experimental and anarchist view of social change while 'politics' obstructs social possibilities. But when science becomes a legitimating ideology for the abuse of power, and a source of techniques to be used in the interests of power, then the pretensions of 'science' may be opposed by the political tradition of creativity and freedom (for a persuasive attack on 'scientism' in the name of political values see, Bernard Crick, *In Defence of Politics*).

The confusions of the debate between 'science' and 'politics' arise because both have been divorced from their original humanistic context. Greek philosophy was imbued with conviction that in human affairs it is essential to retain moderation and balance. If men succumb to the temptation to assume godlike powers through an overweening pride, then just and inevitable retribution will follow. The relevance of this principle (which is both a moral and an aesthetic principle) has been demonstrated in modern science—in, for example, the splitting of the atom. Its relevance to politics is equally obvious. While Greek city states were as prone as most régimes to the 'arrogance of power' their view of politics was informed by the sense that moderation was an inherent political value. Moreover, politics in this sense was based primarily on speech, and so on reasoned persuasion, not on force; on the collective action of equals, not the enforced obedience of slaves.

This picture of politics among a community of citizens naturally undergoes a radical change if politics is understood primarily in relation to the rulers of nation States, within which society is hierarchical and the majority of subjects passive. This is the context assumed by Shakespeare. Machiavelli sketches an outline of politics which includes both the virtues of the citizen in the classical republic, and the machinations of the Prince whose heroic capacity may be demonstrated by the magnitude of his crimes. This blurring of republican politics with princely-power politics has been handed down to us, though for most people the latter image is probably predominant. But a double image of the political sphere creates confusion about the relevance of moral criteria. A tradition of republican politics embodies values which pure power politics may destroy. So the anarchist contention that power politics within nation states is not inevitable can claim support from the classical tradition of politics.

Machiavelli's ideal is Rome with its austere and martial virtues. But even the more diverse and humanistic Athenian ideal of republican 'politics' is not compatible with Tolstoy's Christian morality.

Hannah Arendt has, however, made an interesting concession towards the Tolstoyan view in a recent essay on 'Truth and Politics', though she chooses first a Greek rather than a Christian example. In discussing the influence of the Socratic proposition that 'it is better to suffer wrong than to do wrong' she suggests that the influence this statement has had arises not from philosophical argument, but the power of example—because Socrates staked his life on this truth. She sees this as the only way ethical principles can enter the political realm without distortion. The inspiration of the principle in action encourages imitation, and creates a model which enables us to grasp the principle. It is certainly true that the history of individual conscientious disobedience to the commands of government is understood, and handed down, largely in terms of certain key figures; and one can trace the inspiration of Thoreau and Tolstoy on, for example, Gandhi, who has in turn partially inspired movement of civil disobedience in the United States and Britain.

Tolstoy appeals to the individual conscience and to a morality which claims its validity from a source outside the political sphere, but which often challenges the crimes committed under the label of political necessity. But individual disobedience has its roots also in that very different kind of anarchy which stems from clinging doggedly to one's home, family, health, life and personal enjoyment as long as humanly possible. Despite the apolitical nature of this common ambition, private values do have relevance to politics in encouraging qualities like prudence and caution. These are political virtues for Machiavelli too, but in his context tend to look like pure calculation of risks, and of the risks of those who have, or are gambling for, power. A general respect for the goods of private life suggests a much greater caution about gambling with other peoples' lives. Debunking of heroic pretensions and principles also guards against fanaticism and idolatory and helps to keep politics down to earth.

Not only does commitment to private values have general implications for political policies, it also tends to have implications for personal political action. Men can sometimes build precarious happiness by concentrating on their private welfare; but before the worst disasters of war and tyranny the individual is often most helpless to save himself by being apolitical. Brecht, who often salutes the qualities of tenacious self-preservation, and of dogged obedience to the absurd commands of the powers-that-be, embodied in the Good Soldier Schweik, also emphasizes the necessity of social responsibility. He shows, for example, in *The Resistible Rise of Artura Ui* (about Hitler's rise to power) how social corruption, the narrow interests of those with economic and political power, together with the timidity of the common man, enable Hitler to gain increasingly irresistible power. Alex Comfort, who is sceptical about the values of heroism, is nevertheless convinced in *Art and Social Responsibility* that desire for self preservation must be translated into active resistance: 'From now on, the deserter is every man's friend' (88) and 'You can abolish firing squads only by refusing to serve in them' (85) But this steers dangerously close to heroism.

The Citizen

Indeed, once the apolitical common man begins to pursue the logic of his values and engage in disobedience he begins to find a meeting ground with the individual following the star of his own conscience, especially when the conscientious resister also begins to politicize his stand. Both may seize on the idea of responsible citizenship. Socrates and later Thoreau justified their actions in part on the grounds that they were acting for the real good of their society, and submitted themselves to the laws of that community. Alex Comfort is less concerned with individual civil disobedience in a relatively civilized State, and more with popular and 'underground' resistance in a dictatorship or society mobilized for war. But he also stresses that the criterion is personal responsibility, the safeguarding of freedom by disobedience. A concept of citizenship also fills the gap between an aristocratic code of heroism and the selfish prudence of the commoner pictured by Shakespeare. Citizenship denotes critical judgment and personal responsibility, and is, therefore, opposed to the 'somnambulant heroism' of those who go to war and commit atrocities; at the same time it demands courageous, but where possible prudent, resistance. The model of citizenship also narrows the gap between the political virtues of the ruling Prince—a sense of social responsibility and of social necessities—and the moral standards of the individual conscience.

One of the main tenets of anarchist political theory is, therefore, the belief in the frequent necessity of disobedience to governments and resistance to particular policies. This idea of resistance may be based on a wide range of values: it may be seen primarily as an assertion of original 'political' or republican values against the distorted justifications of power politics; it may stem from a non-political moral commitment; from a sense of artistic or scientific or philosophical responsibility; or from an instinctive and intuitive sense of human responsibility. While these standpoints may often conflict in the values they espouse and the specific actions they encourage, they also tend to overlap and to gain a certain unity from their opposition

to common evils. They also unite in their refusal to accept uncritic-
ally any appeal to morality, idealism or faith designed to justify
various forms of war and oppression. Alex Comfort sums up this
scepticism: 'when they begin to say "Look, injustice," you must
reply, "Whom do you want me to kill?" ' (Art and Social Responsibility, 83).

This commonsense scepticism is intrinsic to the philosophy of
that theorist most concerned to inculcate civil obedience—Hobbes.
But Hobbes directs his attack not against the justifications of governments, but against the independence of conscience, philosophical
questioning, aristocratic heroism, or devotion to the ideal of democratic citizenship, which may all in different ways undermine the
stability of government. As a result Hobbes defends the morality
of the 'tame man' who obeys through fear and prudence. He is not,
however, unaware of the political limitations of this model of the
ideal subject, or of the validity of other values. In the Conclusion of
his Leviathan he discusses those qualities which go to make up a good
citizen of the commonwealth, qualities which are said to be incompatible in one man, but which can be combined through education
and discipline. Two of these incompatibles are courage which dis-
dains death and wounds, and so also inclines men to unsettling the
public peace; and that safe timorousness, which however 'many times
disposeth to the desertion of the public defence'. Hobbes then inserts
an epitaph to the man to whose memory the Leviathan is formally
dedicated:

> There is therefore no such inconsistence of human nature, with
> civil duties, as some think. I have known clearness of judgement
> and largeness of fancy; strength of reason, and graceful elocution;
> a courage for the wars, and a fear for the laws, and all eminently
> in one man; and that was my most noble and honoured friend,
> Mr Sidney Godolphin; who hating no man, nor hated of any,
> was unfortunately slain in the beginning of the late civil war,
> in the public quarrel, by an undiscerned and undiscerning
> hand (461).

The figure of Godolphin which briefly illuminates the Leviathan
also introduces a sense of loss, not only because he personifies the
tragedy of violent death, but because he embodies political values
of active and responsible citizenship. Oakeshott in his essay on 'The
Moral Life in the Writings of Thomas Hobbes' comments:

> Indeed, it seems almost to have been Hobbes's view that men of
> this character are a necessary cause of the civitas; and certainly
> it is only they who, having an adequate motive for doing so, may

be depended upon to defend it when dissension deprives the
sovereign of his power (*Rationalism in Politics*, 293).

The rarity of such qualities, however, leads Hobbes to place his
faith in passive obedience to a sovereignty which men may well call
'tyranny'. Citizenship appears to imply a community of citizens,
which depends on favourable cultural and political forms; conditions
which in many cases are not more favourable now than when
Hobbes wrote. But, as Thomas Mann realized when looking desperately for a possible conjunction of cultural values and political
organization capable of stopping the rise of Hitler in Germany, the
existence of this kind of political responsibility may be essential to
stave off total barbarism. Hobbes's philosophy of the tame man has
often succeeded all too well; while his own type of critical intelligence, and sense of the conditional nature of obedience, have frequently been submerged by the kind of myths and fanaticism he
deplored.

One reason why many anarchists hold on, from their varying
standpoints, to a sense of political or social responsibility, which
transcends or opposes government definitions of what a 'good citizen'
should do, is because they retain a degree of optimism about realizing a better community—here and now in the interstices of the
State, and in the future. This optimism is not facile; in this century
it may at times become desperate. But as Herbert Read once commented : 'The task of the anarchist philosopher is not to prove the
imminence of a Golden Age, but to justify the value of believing in
its possibility' (*Anarchy and Order*, 14).

Conclusion

This study has tried to demonstrate that anarchist ideas are directly related to the more orthodox concepts and concerns of political theory, and closely allied to other major political traditions. It has also attempted to show that anarchism has acquired more, rather than less, relevance in contemporary political, economic and technical conditions. While the last chapter suggested that those forms of anarchism which seem to be least political often, in fact, promote a sense of individual social responsibility. Standing aside from conventionally conceived politics may paradoxically enable anarchists to realize certain values of citizenship, and an ideal of political community, almost lost within the present meaning of 'politics'.

Nevertheless, this standing aside from the political arena entails at the same time a serious theoretical and practical weakness. A pure anarchism cannot fully meet the constitutionalist demand for immediate political responsibility, because it refuses to consider the possible necessity of compromise with the bad to prevent the worse. This form of consistency has its virtues, especially when it takes the form of resistance to State policies in a primarily conformist society; but its value is largely predicated on it being a minority position. Guérin points to the incoherence of the anarchist position on voting (L'Anarchisme, 22–3). He quotes Malatesta, who maintained in relation to the new 'Cartel des Gauches', formed for the May, 1924, French election, that even if some small amount of progress might be achieved through the election, the anarchists should retain their revolutionary purity and boycott the polls. On the other hand, the Bakuninists in the First International had protested that boycotting the polls was not an article of faith but a matter of tactics. The anarchists in Spain oscillated between these two positions, joining with the democratic Parties in 1930 to overthrow Primo de Rivera, counselling abstention in the 1933 general election, and in 1936, though supporting the Popular Front, half-heartedly advising abstention—advice they did not expect to be heeded.

Secondly, anarchism has not yet been able to meet the Marxist demand for political effectiveness; and continuous failure can only be translated into a form of glory by appealing to non-political values. The nature of anarchist theory means that in any important political crisis individuals who seek to influence events by accepting

a leadership position—for example, in a 'government'—are open to
charges of gross inconsistency or treachery to the cause. Similarly at
the level of mass action anarchists prepared to sink their differences
in a united front, or to ally themselves with a popular movement,
may be torn between the importance of action and maintaining their
principles. During the Russian Revolution and Civil War anarchists
were split not only on the question of whether to support the
Bolsheviks, but on their attitude to the popular peasant 'anarchism'
of Makhno's movement. As a guide to action Marxism has an advant-
age, since it refrains from imposing abstract and inflexible principles
upon political evaluation of a total situation.

Nevertheless, tactical flexibility has its own traps, and one of the
most important contributions of anarchism to political theory is
its critique of Marxist 'success', and insistence on relating means to
ends. Emma Goldman comments in *My Disillusionment with Russia*
that she came to realize that the Bolsheviks believed that the end
justifies *all* means:

> Any suggestion of the value of human life, quality of character,
> the importance of revolutionary integrity as the basis of a new
> social order, was repudiated as 'bourgeois' sentimentality (70).

Anarchists themselves are split between those who regard all forms
of violence as brutalizing, and believe violent means are incompatible
with the goal of an anarchist society; and those who think that a
degree of violence may often be necessary, or inevitable. Emma
Goldman, who is in the latter category, distinguishes between types
of 'violence':

> It is quite one thing to employ violence in combat, as a means of
> defence. It is quite another thing to make a principle of terrorism,
> to institutionalize it, to assign it the most vital place in the social
> struggle. Such terrorism begets counter-revolution and in turn
> itself becomes counter-revolutionary (xix).

Within the anarchist tradition there is not only a critique of the
abuse of power after a revolution, but an important criticism of the
romantic theory of revolution—the belief that a revolution which
breaks decisively with the past will automatically promote a new
social era. Instead it is urged that building up the institutions of a
new society is a long term process, which must be started here and
now. A revolution which cannot build on creative tendencies and
institutional forms already in existence is likely to become increasingly destructive, and resurrect coercive centralized power. This
approach goes beyond Stirner's distinction between a politically
directed 'revolution' leading to a new State, and a spontaneous in-

surrection destroying all political power; and it underlines the
dangers of the Bakuninist ideal of rebellion. It is one of the contributions to anarchist thought made by Landauer, who, drawing on
both Proudhon and Kropotkin, appeals to the communal traditions
of the past. 'The radical reformer will find nothing to reform except
what is there' (Buber, *Paths in Utopia*, 49). Landauer's aim is in
Buber's phrase 'a revolutionary conservation'. But it can be understood with Landauer's 'conservative' overtones. Landauer himself
looked to the new working class institutions of the co-operatives
and trade unions :

> We want to bring the Co-operatives, which are socialist in form
> without socialist content, and the trade-unions, which are valour
> without avail—to Socialism, to great experiments (54).

The distinction made by Landauer between a social principle and
a political principle suggests two important modes of action appropriate to anarchism. One is to build up independent communities
and organizations within the existing State, and so create a new
society in embryo, and an alternative power base. The other is to
erode the power of those at the top—a power in reality springing
from the co-operative action of the social group as a whole—by
withdrawing co-operation and refusing to obey orders. If non-co-operation were adopted on a mass scale the 'power' of the men at the top
would cease to exist. Both these approaches are wholly consistent
with anarchist principles, and both are potentially effective. The
snag is that both must be linked to some form of popular movement
if they are to have immediate impact; and to achieve ultimate success
they must be part of a strategy which can force changes in
policy at a national level, and eventually overthrow the powers-
that-be. Hence both approaches may still require political compro-
mises.

The relevance of both approaches when anarchism is linked to an
existing movement was demonstrated by the development of syndicalism. Trade union organization provided an institutional base which
could be strengthened in immediate struggles, extended to constructive experiments like producers' co-operatives, and could be seen
as an alternative administrative framework in the future. Trade union
activity could link people's immediate interests to wider long term
goals. The strike provided a potent means of direct action, which
could be supplemented by boycotts and sabotage; and trade union
struggle could be extended to the seizure and control of the factories.
The general strike held out the promise of achieving specific political
goals, like prevention of war, and of ultimately achieving the overthrow of the government and the capitalist class. Syndicalism has

built-in dangers of authoritarian organizational tendencies, or of trade union reformism arising out of immediate demands for higher wages, shorter hours and better conditions. As Nicolas Walter comments (Anarchy No. 100). these problems are not in themselves an argument against syndicalism; he criticizes it rather for its Marxist emphasis on exclusively working class militancy (178).

Another area in which anarchism has come into its own, and can point to striking temporary successes, is in that tradition of popular revolutionary experience which has thrown up the organizational system of workers and communal councils. This tendency, which can be traced to the French Revolution, has been demonstrated recently in Hungary and Poland in 1956, and in France in May 1968. With the exception of Spain in the 1930s, the council system has not been directly inspired by an organized anarchist movement, and conscious anarchist influence has often been totally absent. The symbol of the communal council, or local soviet, has been incorporated also into both official and unofficial Marxism. More surprisingly, it has certain attractions for constitutionalist theorists. De Jouvenel, drawing on Montesquieu, creates his book, Power, an abstract outline of a confederation of councils as an alternative to party-based parliamentary democracy. Since the emergence of the workers' soviets in Hungary in November 1956 Hannah Arendt has explored this approach to democracy in detail in On Revolution. But in her constitutionalist version the councils are assigned an exclusively 'political' role and deemed inappropriate to management of industry, and so are denuded of their specifically socialist character. Whilst under Marxism the councils tend to be divested of their truly democratic character—rapidly the case in Russia after 1917; and partly true today in Yugoslavia, where they are still to some extent subordinate to the Party as well as to the central government. Anarchists can, therefore, perhaps claim that their theory is more in tune with the aspirations which have been shown by the movements which have embraced this form of social organization.

One important respect in which anarchism appears to represent the embryonic institutional ideas of the council movements is in their advocacy of confederation built up from below as an alternative to the centralized power of the State, a power making at most concessions towards deconcentration of administrative authority. The idea of confederation put forward successively by the major anarchist theorists provides a potential bridge between the anarchism adapted to a small community and the need for co-ordination in modern industrial society.

The promise of confederation lies, however, partly in its ambiguity. For example, though Bakunin follows Proudhon in emphasizing the organizational role of the local commune, as well as of producers' associations, this may not be entirely consistent with his stress on large scale industry. On the one hand, there arise questions, which have tended to divide anarchists and syndicalists, about the relative role of the local commune and industry-based trade unions. On the other, wider questions of economic planning arise. Some of these problems may be resolved by voluntary agreement on standardization, as in the popular anarchist example of inter-continental railway networks. Some may be resolved by strictly functional delegation to specialized bodies, or by the creation of reserve emergency powers subject to political restrictions. And given the noteworthy failures of over-centralized planning it would be rash to dismiss the possibility of economic co-ordination on a confederal basis. But there are still major questions about the size of the basic units involved and about the mechanics of communication and decision making.

There are also questions about the permanency and formality of the organization involved. A confederal constitution and planning organization tend to conflict with Kropotkin's emphasis on no formal 'government' and on spontaneous co-ordination and federation. They would also conflict with the four principles of anarchist organization suggested by Colin Ward: that organization should be voluntary, functional, temporary and small. His article on 'The Organization of Anarchy' successfully shows that giving full scope to different talents and individual initiative may work much better than a standardized and hierarchial structure; and he illustrates how 'spontaneous order' can emerge out of apparent chaos. Ward also refutes the belief (voiced by Engels) that 'authority' is necessary to run a ship or a factory, by reference to the gang system among workers in Coventry, and composite working of the Durham coal fields, which both demonstrate that self-regulating groups of workers can promote high productivity without conventional supervision (Krimerman and Perry, *Patterns of Anarchy*, 393-5). But the article does not show how confederation can be based on his four principles. Indeed confederation has usually been regarded as a compromise solution by anarchists. Proudhon sought to limit the scope and permanence of individual authority, and to maintain the principle of confederation by retaining more power at the local and intermediary levels than is delegated to the centre. As a compromise with constitutionalist or socialist approaches to politics, the idea of confederation has immediate relevance to political theory.

Whether anarchism will produce more than suggestive ideas for a theory of politics, or whether a specifically anarchist movement will ever achieve success, are both open to considerable doubt. On the other hand, anarchist ideas may be important in the reinterpretation of liberalism and socialism, and may be partially realized in the aims of activities of popular movements. Since anarchism is in essence the least sectarian of doctrines, effective diffusion of anarchist influence might constitute its ultimately most valuable contribution to politics.

Suggestions for further reading

A number of introductory books on anarchism have recently appeared in paperback:

GEORGE WOODCOCK, Anarchism, Penguin Books

IRVING L. HOROWITZ, (ed.), The Anarchists, Dell Publishing Co.

LEONARD I. KRIMERMAN and LEWIS PERRY, (eds.), Patterns of Anarchy, Doubleday

Many of the writings of anarchist theorists have not been translated into English, or are out of print. However the following are available in paperback:

PIERRE-JOSEPH PROUDHON, Selected Writings of Pierre-Joseph Proudhon (ed. Stewart Edwards), Macmillan

MICHAEL BAKUNIN, The Political Philosophy of Bakunin (ed. G. P. Maximoff), The Free Press of Glencoe

PETER KROPOTKIN, Memoirs of a Revolutionist, Dover Books

LEO TOLSTOY, Tolstoy's Writings on Civil Disobedience and Non-violence, Signet Books

A number of detailed historical studies are also now available:

PAUL AVRICH, The Russian Anarchists, Oxford University Press

GERALD BRENAN, The Spanish Labyrinth, Cambridge University Press (by no means exclusively on the anarchists, but includes useful material)

JOHN WOMACK, Zapata and the Mexican Revolution, Thames & Hudson

GEOFFREY OSTERGAARD, The Gentle Anarchists,
(on the present Gandhian movement in India)

One of the best guides to literature being published, and to anarchist theory past and present is the monthly journal Anarchy, published by Freedom Press, 84b Whitechapel High Street, London, E.1.

Bibliography

Anarchy, Freedom Press, No. 98 (April 1969) No. 91 (September 1968), No. 94 (December 1968) No. 96 (February 1969)

ARENDT, HANNAH, (1959), *The Human Condition*, Doubleday, Anchor Books, New York

ARENDT, HANNAH, (1963), *On Revolution*, Faber and Faber

ARENDT, HANNAH, (1958), *The Origins of Totalitarianism*, Allen and Unwin

ARENDT, HANNAH, 'Truth and Politics', *Philosophy, Politics and Society*, Third Series (eds. P. Laslett and W. G. Runciman), (1967), Basil Blackwell

BAKUNIN, MICHAEL, (circa 1915) *God and the State*, Mother Earth Publishing Association, New York

BAKUNIN, MICHAEL, (1950), *Marxism, Freedom and the State*, (ed. K. J. Kenafick), Freedom Press

BAKUNIN, MICHAEL, (1964), *The Political Philosophy of Bakunin*, (ed. G. P. Maximoff), The Free Press of Glencoe, Free Press Paperbacks, New York

BALDWIN, JAMES, (1965), *Notes of a Native Son*, Corgi Books

BARKER, ERNEST, (1951), *Principles of Social and Political Theory*, Oxford University Press Paperbacks

BENDIX, REINHARD, (1966), *Max Weber*, Methuen University Paperbacks

BERKMAN, ALEXANDER, (1964), *ABC of Anarchism*, Freedom Press

BERKMAN, ALEXANDER, (1953), *The Bolshevik Myth*, Livenight, New York

BERKMAN, ALEXANDER, 'Kronstadt: The Final Act in Russian Anarchism', *The Anarchists* (ed. Irving L. Horowitz), (1964), Dell, New York

BOGNAR, JOSZEF, 'Gandhi's Hundredth Birthday', *The New Hungarian Quarterly*, Vol. XI, No. 37, (Spring 1970)

BRAMSTEDT, E. K., (1945), *Dictatorship and Political Police*, Kegan Paul, Trench and Trubner

BRENAN, GERALD, (1967), *The Spanish Labyrinth*, Cambridge University Press Paperback

BUBER, MARTIN, (1949), *Paths in Utopia*, Routledge & Kegan Paul

BUBER, MARTIN, (1957), *Pointing the Way*, Routledge & Kegan Paul

CAMUS, ALBERT, (1962), *The Rebel*, Penguin Books

COLE, G. D. H., (1961), *A History of Socialist Thought*, vols. 1–5, Macmillan

COLTMAN, IRENE, (1962), *Private Men and Public Causes*, Faber & Faber

COMFORT, ALEX, (1946), *Art and Social Responsibility*, Falcon Press

COMFORT, ALEX, (1950), *Authority and Delinquency in the Modern State*, Routledge & Kegan Paul

CRICK, BERNARD, (1964), *In Defence of Politics*, Penguin Books

DE JOUVENEL, BERTRAND, (1948), *Power*, Hutchinson & Co.

DE JOUVENEL, BERTRAND, (1963), *The Pure Theory of Politics*, Cambridge

University Press

DE MAUNY, ERIK, (1969), *Russian Prospect*, Macmillan

DE TOCQUEVILLE, ALEXIS, (1951), *Democracy in America*, 2 vols., Alfred A. Knopf, New York

DE TOCQUEVILLE, ALEXIS, (1955), *The Old Régime and the French Revolution*, Doubleday, Anchor Books, New York

DRINNON, RICHARD, (1961), *Rebel in Paradise*, University of Chicago Press

DURKHEIM, EMILE, (1962), *Socialism*, Collier Books, New York

FEUERBACH, LUDWIG, (1957), *The Essence of Christianity*, Harper Torchbooks, New York

GODWIN, WILLIAM, (1946), *Enquiry Concerning Political Justice*, 2 vols., University of Toronto Press

GODWIN, WILLIAM, (1949), *Political Justice: A Reprint of the Essays on Property* (ed. H. S. Salt), Allen & Unwin

GOLDMAN, EMMA, (undated), *Anarchism and Other Essays*, Modern Publishers, Indore, India

GOLDMAN, EMMA, (1925), *My Disillusionment with Russia*, C. W. Daniel

GOODMAN, PAUL, (1962), *Drawing the Line*, Random House, New York

GOODMAN, PAUL, (1965), *People or Personnel*, Random House, New York

GOODMAN, PAUL, (1964), *Utopian Essays and Practical Proposals*, Vintage Books, New York

GOODMAN, PAUL AND PERCIVAL, (1960), *Communitas*, Vintage Books, New York

GRINDROD, MURIEL, (1968), *Italy*, Ernest Benn

GUÉRIN, DANIEL, (1965), *L'Anarchisme*, Gallimard, Paris

HOBBES, THOMAS, (1960), *Leviathan*, (ed. Michael Oakeshott), Basil Blackwell

HOBSBAWN, ERIC, (1969), *Bandits*, Weidenfeld & Nicolson

KOLAKOWSKI, LESZEK, (1969), *Marxism and Beyond*, Pall Mall Press

KROPOTKIN, P., (1896), *Anarchism: Its Philosophy and Ideal*, Freedom Press

KROPOTKIN, P., (1968), *The Conquest of Bread*, Benjamin Blom, New York and London

KROPOTKIN, P., (1895), *The Commune of Paris*, Freedom Press

KROPOTKIN, P., (1901), *Fields, Factories and Workshops*, Swan Sonnenschein

KROPOTKIN, P., (1886), *Law and Authority*, International Publishing Co.

KROPOTKIN, P., (1906), *Memoirs of a Revolutionist*, Swan Sonnenschein

KROPOTKIN, P., (1923), *Modern Science and Anarchism*, Freedom Press

KROPOTKIN, P., (1946), *The State: Its Historic Role*, Freedom Press

LANDAUER, GUSTAV, (1896), *Social Democracy in Germany*, published at 127 Ossulston Street, London

LAVRIN, JANKO, (1948), *Tolstoy: An Approach*, Methuen

LENIN, V. I., (undated), *The State and Revolution*, Foreign Languages Publishing House, Moscow

LENIN, V. I., (undated), *What Is To Be Done?* Foreign Languages Publishing House, Moscow

LUKACS, GEORG, (1964), *Essays on Thomas Mann*, Merlin Press

MALATESTA, ERRICO, (1965), *Errico Malatesta: His Life and Ideas* (ed. Vernon Richards), Freedom Press

MARX, KARL, AND ENGELS, FREDERICK, (1965), *The German Ideology*, Lawrence & Wishart

MARX, KARL, AND ENGELS, FREDERICK, (undated), *Selected Correspondence*, Foreign Languages Publishing House, Moscow

MARX, KARL, AND ENGELS, FREDERICK, (1968), *Selected Works*, Progress Publishers, Moscow

MAXWELL, GAVIN, (1959) *The Ten Pains of Death*, Longmans

MCDERMOTT, JOHN, 'Knowledge is Power', *The Nation*, Vol. 208, No. 15 (14 April 1969)

MOLNAR, GEORGE, 'The Anarchist Past', *Anarchy*, No. 28 (June 1963)

MORRIS, WILLIAM, (1968), *William Morris: Selected Writings and Designs* (ed. Asa Briggs), Penguin Books

MORTON, H. W., 'Randloph Bourne vs the State', *Anarchy*, No. 31 (September 1963)

NOMAD, MAX, (1939), *Apostles of Revolution*, Secker & Warburg

OAKESHOTT, MICHAEL, (1967), *Rationalism and Politics*, Methuen

ORTEGA Y GASSET, JOSE, (1961), *The Revolt of the Masses*, Allen & Unwin, Unwin Books

ORWELL, GEORGE, (1964), *Homage to Catalonia*, Penguin Books

ORWELL, GEORGE, 'Lear, Tolstoy and the Fool', *Inside the Whale and Other Essays*, (1962), Penguin Books

OSTERGAARD, GEOFFREY, 'The Relevance of Syndicalism', *Anarchy*, No. 28, (June 1963)

PRESTHUS, ROBERT, 'The Social Dysfunctions of Organization', *The Anarchists*, (ed. Irving L. Horowitz), (1964), Dell Publishing Co., New York

PROUDHON, P. – J., (1863), *Du Principe Federatif*, E. Dentu, Paris

PROUDHON, P. – J., (1851), *Idée Generale de la Revolution au XIX Siècle*, Garnier Frères, Paris

PROUDHON, P. – J., (1852), *La Revolution Sociale*, Garnier Frères, Paris

READ, HERBERT, (1954), *Anarchy and Order*, Faber & Faber

ROCKER, RUDOLPH, (undated), *Anarcho-Syndicalism*, Modern Publishers, Indore, India

SAMPSON, R. V., (1965), *Equality and Power*, Heinemann

STIRNER, MAX, (1963), *The Ego and His Own*, Libertarian Book Club, New York

THOREAU, HENRY DAVID, 'Civil Disobedience', *The Pacifist Conscience*, (ed. Peter Mayer), (1966), Penguin Books

TOLSTOY, LEO, (1948), *Essays from Tula*, Sheppard Press

TOLSTOY, LEO, (1966), *Resurrection*, Penguin Books

TUCHMAN, BARBARA, 'Anarchism in France', *The Anarchists*, (ed. Irving L. Horowitz) (1964), Dell Publishing Co., New York

TUCKER, BENJAMIN R., (1911), *State Socialism and Anarchism*, A. C. Fifield

WALTER, NICOLAS, 'About Anarchism', *Anarchy*, No. 100 (June 1969)

WARD, COLIN, 'The Organization of Anarchy', *Patterns of Anarchy*, (eds. Leonard I. Krimerman and Lewis Perry), (1966), Doubleday, Anchor

Books, New York

WARD, COLIN, 'The State and Society', *Anarchy*, No. 14 (April 1962)

WHITAKER, BEN, (1964), *The Police*, Penguin Books

WILDE, OSCAR, (1912), *The Soul of Man under Socialism*, Arthur L. Humphreys

WILLIAMS, PHILIP, (1954), *Politics in Post-War France*, Longmans, Green & Co.

WISE, DAVID, AND ROSS, THOMAS B., (1965), *The Invisible Government*, Jonathan Cape

WOODCOCK, GEORGE, (1963), *Anarchism*, Penguin Books

71 72 73 74   12 11 10 9 8 7 6 5 4 3 2 1